THEATRE ARTS

workbook

ROSEMARY LINNELL

Hodder & Stoughton

LONDON SYDNEY AUCKLAND TORONTO

British Library Cataloguing in Publication Data
Linnell, Rosemary
  Theatre arts workbook : a student book for those studying
  drama.
  1. Stagecraft
  I. Title
  792.02

  ISBN 0–340–54110–5

First published 1991

Typeset by Wearside Tradespools, Fulwell, Sunderland.
Printed in Great Britain for the educational publishing division of Hodder and Stoughton Ltd, Mill Road, Dunton Green, Sevenoaks, Kent by St Edmundsbury Press.

CONTENTS

INTRODUCTION

The term 'Theatre Arts' covers a very exciting and interesting blend of technical ability and imagination, and anyone who takes part in a Theatre Arts course is probably drawn to it for that very reason.

Naturally, jobs in the theatre are often highly specialised, and someone who becomes an expert in stage lighting may never want to direct actors, just as the director of a stage musical may never be required to wire up a plug. The best lighting designers, however, will understand all the demands made upon the director of a play and will be able to contribute to the overall effect and interpretation of the piece, just as the best directors will be able to think in terms of the technical value as well as the effectiveness of the lighting equipment that is available. A stage production very quickly becomes a team activity, and every member of that team needs to be not only aware, but also knowledgeable, about the work of every other member of the team.

The purpose of this book is to provide an outline of most of the techniques, skills and creative processes required to mount a theatrical performance. There are times when it will be necessary for a group to carry out some of the tasks by working together, although there are also many practical exercises and opportunities for individual thought and planning – just as in the theatre there are long periods of preparation and private thinking as well as times for hard practical work, collaboration and sharing ideas. By working through all the skills in this workbook, and tackling the assignments at the end of each section, a student should be thoroughly equipped to become part of a production team with a full understanding of everything that goes to make a good performance. After that it will be up to every student to negotiate with the course leader which skills to offer for a more specialised study.

Throughout the book there is an assumption that the student of Theatre Arts is already acquainted with the basic groundwork of drama and theatre, is used to working as part of a team in school or college, and is equipped with sufficient understanding to know that the time has come for more specialised work. This is an opportunity to gain some further skills and to be able to undertake some practical projects alone, or in groups, without the pressures of the school play or the college production.

SPACE

From the street corner to the most fully equipped drama studio, the nature of any performance area will affect both the actors and the audience to a marked degree. It will even determine the shaping of the piece to be performed, since, although no performance space is forever fixed and unchanging, it will possess certain characteristics which will suit some styles better than others. Everyone who is going to work in the space needs to know and understand its potential, in terms of the relationship between actor and audience. The best way to get to know the limitations as well as the assets of a space is to make a really detailed plan.

There may already be a ground plan of the drama room or theatre space in which you work, so there is nothing to be gained by making another. However, a detailed and absolutely accurate plan is essential as a basis for all practical work. Each department in the theatre team needs something to work from, so it may be necessary to measure up the floor space as well as to determine the height and position of any fixed and unchangeable ceiling bars, pillars, doors, windows and changes in floor level. In any case, the plan should be checked against your observations of the space itself.

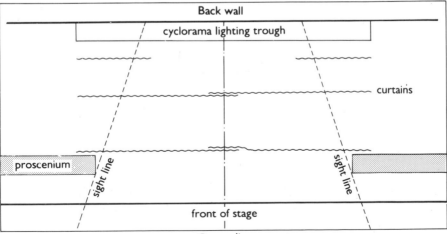

Sample groundplan of a proscenium stage

After studying the variety of actor/audience relationships described here you should be able to fit many, if not all of them into your own working environment. If you are faced with fixed seats and a permanently raised stage there may be fewer options available, but there will nevertheless be some alternatives to the picture-frame format.

The picture-frame stage

As its name suggests, the picture-frame stage is designed to make the audience into spectators and the actors into part of a picture that is only seen from the front. Actors often refer to the audience as being 'out front'; they speak 'out front' and the auditorium is the 'front of house'.

A proscenium stage

Although this seems a very traditional way of staging, it has a relatively recent history. The effect of being spectators of a living picture depends upon the audience being almost invisible and silent, which in turn means that there has to be a completely dark auditorium contrasted with a brightly lit stage. This has only been possible in the theatre since the introduction of lighting controls, first with gas lighting in the early nineteenth century and then with electric light. A curtain often conceals the stage picture from the audience and, when it rises and the front-of-house lights are dimmed, all attention is focused on to the stage picture.

Another way of describing this form of actor–audience relationship is 'the fourth wall convention'. It is as though the actors are in another room, next door to the audience, except that the wall that separates them has been removed. The audience can see 'through the fourth wall' while the actors behave as though there is no audience there and as though this is a 'slice of life' taking place in their normal living space.

The majority of theatres built at the end of the nineteenth century and in the first half of the twentieth century were intended for this type of performance. Mostly they are large theatres, designed to hold large numbers of people. In such an environment it is easy to lose one's own identity and to identify with the actor's portrayal of a realistic life-style.

It might be worthwhile considering what could be the major problems with this type of theatre, both from the actors' point of view and from that of the audience.

Assignments

I For the best impression of what this style of theatre can convey and what kind of setting is most effective, make a model of an imaginary room in a box and then cut a hole in one side to make a frame. If possible, put a lid on the box (with holes to admit light) and look through the frame at your room. What happens if you look through from slightly above? From the side, or below? If this were a stage setting, are there changes that would have to be made to ensure that it could be seen to its best advantage?

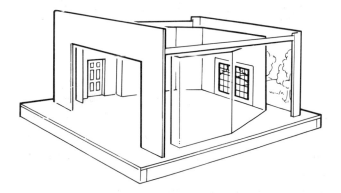

A model of a room set in a box

2 Use the ground plan to arrange your performance area as a picture-frame stage. Are there advantages in such an arrangement? In practical terms, is there room for entrances and exits and for arranging the audience so that everyone can see through the frame? If the area is already set out in this way, examine the arrangement of lighting equipment, exits, and the height of the stage, and the placing of such things as the curtain and sound controls, stage management desk and so on. How far is it possible to maintain the illusion that the audience is eavesdropping on a realistic situation?

Proscenium stage

Sometimes a picture-frame stage is called a proscenium stage. The name is derived from classical theatre when the acting area was constructed in front of a temple (called the 'skene'), from which we get the term 'scene'. 'Pro' means 'in front of', therefore 'pro-scenium' denotes that area in front of the scenery. As early as the court performances in seventeenth century Europe, there was a scene area with a frame to define it and to hide the stage machinery, and an acting area, with entrances on either side, set in an elaborate proscenium arch which also contained 'boxes' or balconied windows above the doors.

The Old Price Riot at Covent Garden in 1763, during a performance of Artaxerxes *by Thomas Arne*

To light the actors, chandeliers hung from the top of the arch, and other candles or lamps lit the audience. Versions of this form of staging lasted from the seventeenth to the early years of the present century, and the picture-frame stage simply puts the actor finally and firmly into the scene area behind the proscenium arch and lights them both together, leaving the audience in darkness.

Multi-purpose hall stage with fixed seats. The effect is that of an end stage with a proscenium

End stage

If the picture-frame is removed altogether from your room setting, you are left with an open stage which still has the audience on one side of it. The actors still face out front and speak out front, but some of the illusion of the fourth wall convention is gone. It may now be possible to see beyond the edge of the scene area. It will certainly be possible to see over the top. If it were a full-size theatre building, the stage lighting and actors and stage-hands waiting at the side of the stage would at least be dimly visible to the audience. There would be no doubt that the audience were attending a stage performance, even though they might still be sitting in anonymous darkness.

Many of the older theatres have been adapted to take account of this theatrical environment by having most of the stage lighting and sound equipment in full view of the audience and by bringing some of the action and setting in front of the picture frame. Actors may also address the audience directly, thus avoiding any sense that the performance represents 'a slice of life'.

The Mermaid Theatre, London

Many theatres are purpose-built with an end stage; it is often the form that is chosen for studio plays or improvisations since it is very direct and quick to set up, and poses few problems concerning lighting, setting and 'facing the audience'.

Assignment

Either on your plan or in the actual space available, try out different arrangements to provide an end stage. Look for the actors' entrances; the best arrangement for providing scenery or a setting for a performance; whether the audience needs to be raised in order to see;

and whether it is possible to light the actors satisfactorily. Where would you put the lighting and sound operators? Would the stage management be seen? Is it possible to have an end stage arrangement across a corner? What might this contribute to the performance?

Apron, thrust and open stages

I Apron stage

When some of the old picture-frame theatres were adapted to bring the actors forward so that they could talk directly to the audience, the acting area was built out like an apron, jutting over what had originally been the orchestra pit. The term apron stage is also sometimes given to any stage which juts forward into the auditorium, but there are other, more precise terms for purpose-built stages of this type.

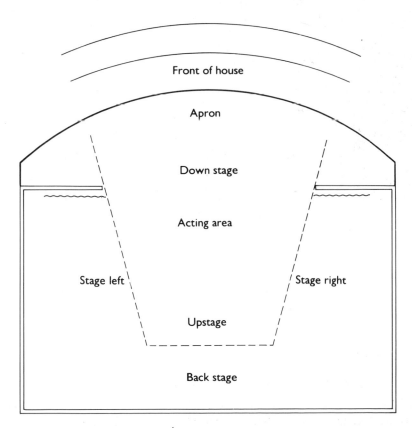

An apron stage

2 Thrust stage

The projecting front of an apron stage can sometimes be thrust out into the auditorium. The true thrust stage, however, does not jut forward from the scene area. A thrust stage usually consists of a high, rectangular platform without scenery, having audience at the sides as well as in front, with entrances on the fourth side. In some ways, The Swan Playhouse of Shakespeare's day resembles a thrust stage.

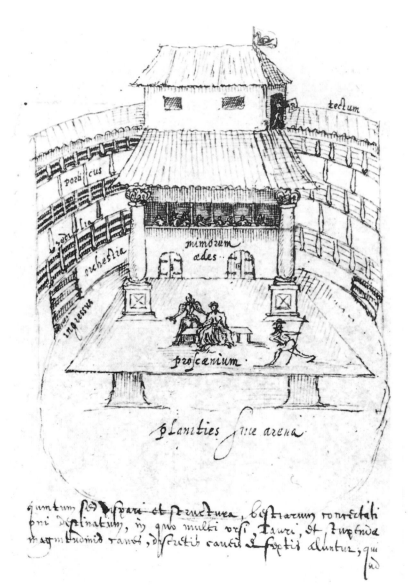

The Swan Playhouse

A thrust stage

3   Open stage

A stage where the audience surrounds the acting area, either in a curve or in straight lines, leaving only one side for entrances, is commonly known as an open stage. The only difference between an open and a thrust stage is that an open stage may be either on the same level as the audience, slightly raised or even lower than the front row of seats. There is very little opportunity for any kind of stage setting other than a few pieces of furniture. The stage is open and merges into the auditorium.

The Chichester Festival Theatre: an open stage

Assignment

The best way of establishing the uses and limitations of any kind of open or thrust stage is to try out different arrangements of the audience during a rehearsal or improvisation session. Discuss the merits and disadvantages of an open acting area with the actors as well as those people watching. Look at the space from the point of view of someone who would have to light it. Are there problems? Where would be the best place to have the stage management and other technical crews during a performance?

Theatre in the round

The logical development from the open stage is to have the audience all round the acting area. In many ways this could be seen as being more realistic, since in real life there is no front or back to our activities, the world is all around us. The moment, however, that a focus of attention is required in order to make oneself heard or for something to be clearly seen, then the audience in the street or market place usually forms itself in front of or to the side of the focus of activity. Theatre in the round is not necessarily the most natural form of theatre anywhere in the world, but there are advantages in a small circle of people making close contact with the actor.

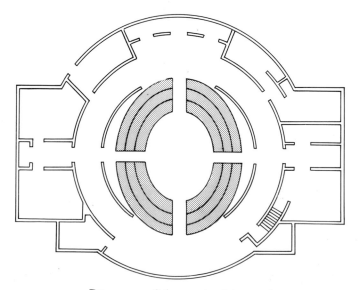

Diagram of theatre in the round

Le Théâtre en Rond de Paris, founded by Paquita Claude and André Villiers in 1954

Assignment

Try the effect of having an audience in a circle around a group of performers. What are the advantages? What are the problems? Do the actors have to change their style of performance? Do they make easy contact with the audience?

Arena stage

Arena stages, like theatre in the round, also have the audience surrounding the stage, but far from the intimacy of theatre in the round, an arena is the largest form of acting area it is possible to have and still allow everyone to see and hear. An arena stage, by virtue of its size, is the type of theatre space that demands large-scale performances and an element of procession or ritual, where movement and action are more important than conversation or subtle characterisation.

A circus arena

Assignment

It may not be possible to try out an arena stage, even on the plan of your acting area. There may, however, be a large building locally, such as a sports hall or even an open space outdoors, where it might be possible to stage a large-scale performance or at least to try out ideas that might be feasible in such a space. It may be possible to visit an arena space where some activity such as ice-skating is going on. Imagine staging a theatre performance there. What are the virtues of the space? What difficulties might you encounter and how would you get over them?

Multi-stages and promenade stages

I Multi-stages

So far, each of the stages under consideration has existed as a single focus for the audience, but it is possible to hold a performance with more than one stage in use at the same time. There are so many possible combinations of acting areas – on opposite sides, one above the other or in a long row, for example – that it is usual to call them all multi-stages and to distinguish only one type for special mention. The pageant stages of the medieval mystery plays consisted of processional wagons, each with its own particular tableau mounted on it, which were drawn up alongside high scaffold platforms in the street or market place. The audience would then stand round to see the performance on the scaffold and occasionally on the wagon-car itself.

Fouquet miniature showing a form of multi-staging

The Valenciennes mystery plays in a multi-stage setting

2   Promenade stages

A promenade performance is different from all the others in this list, in that there is usually no separation between actors and audience. To this extent it can hardly be called a stage, since the audience are milling around, walking, perching or standing about while the actors have to create a space, or series of spaces in which to perform. The attention of the spectators is gained by using spotlights or a commanding voice or by sending someone ahead to make room.

A promenade performance: The Poor Man's Friend *by Howard Barker, directed by Ann Jellicoe*

Assignments

I   The principle of multiple staging is easier to understand by experience than by reading or studying diagrams. Experiment by having individual actors attract attention to themselves when surrounded by an audience and then conduct a scene, or piece of action in the centre of a group. Does the audience shift position in order to see? Is it easier to use raised areas? The following few lines from a traditional mummers' play may serve as a starting point. Try them out and notice how the changes of focus are achieved.

THE MUMMERS' PLAY

[*Enter the* PRESENTER]

PRESENTER.   I open the door, I enter in;
I hope your favour we shall win.
Stir up the fire and strike a light,
And see my merry boys act to-night.
Whether we stand or whether we fall,
We'll do our best to please you all.

[*Enter the actors, and stand in a clump*]

PRESENTER.   Room, room, brave gallants all,
Pray give us room to rhyme;
We're come to show activity,
  This merry Christmas time;
Activity of youth,
Activity of age,
The like was never seen
  Upon a common stage.
And if you don't believe what I say,
Step in St. George – and clear the way.

[*Enter* ST. GEORGE]

ST. GEORGE.   In come I, Saint George,
The man of courage bold;
With my broad axe and sword
I won a crown of gold.

Can you devise further strategies to pass the focus of action from one part of the space to another? Try focusing attention without using speech.

2 In the following extract from *The Love Girl and the Innocent*, the action focuses on a large number of different people who are spread over a wide area. Try staging it as a promenade scene. Discuss with the audience the effect the scene has when staged in this way.

Extract from *The Love Girl and the Innocent* by Alexander Solzhenitsyn

KOLODEY.   All right, those who have been examined, single file, quick march!

[*The prisoners quickly begin to climb into the back of the lorry, pushing each other aside.*]

ESCORT-GUARD SERGEANT.   [*He is standing right in the back of the lorry behind a protective grille, armed with a sub-machine gun.*]   Sit down! Hurry up and sit down! On the floor, not on your bags! Don't turn round! Face the rear! No talking!

KOLODEY [*to* KOSTYA].   Who's missing?

KOSTYA.   Here are the last three. Hurry up, slowcoaches!

[GONTOIR, GRANYA *and* SHUROCHKA *emerge from behind the hut on the left.*]

ESCORT-GUARD SERGEANT.   Gop . . . Gop. . . .

GONTOIR.   Gontoir, Camille Leopoldovich, born 1890, Article 58, paragraph one A stroke nineteen. Ten years.

ESCORT-GUARD SERGEANT.   Take your hat off then!

[GONTOIR *bares his silvery head. The sergeant compares him with the photograph on the cover of his file.*]

You don't look much like your picture . . . All right, on you go.

[GONTOIR *clambers into the lorry.*]

Soykina!

SHUROCHKA [*fussing over her belongings*].   Soykina, Alexandra Pavlovna, Article 58, paragraph twelve. Ten years.

[*She is almost crying. Her things are too heavy for her. There is no one to help her. Finally* KOSTYA *heaves her luggage into the back of the lorry.*]

ESCORT-GUARD SERGEANT.   Zybina!

GRANYA [*her voice clear and angry*].   Agrafena Mikhailovna, born 1920, Article 136. Ten years.

GAI [*shouting from the work area*].   Good-bye, Granya!

GRANYA [*shouts*].   Good-bye, Pavel!

GAI.   Write to me!

GRANYA.   It's too late!

GAI.   Don't give in, Granya!

GRANYA.   I won't!

KOLODEY [*stepping in front of her*].   Stop that! [*Taunting her.*] Don't want to leave your lover behind, is that what's the matter?

GRANYA [*shouting over his head*].   Watch out for Khomich. He's a squealer! I'm sure he is!

WARDRESS.   Shut your face, little bitch. You'll get a rifle butt in the teeth!

[GRANYA *and* SHUROCHKA *disappear behind the side of the lorry.*]

Further assignments on the general use of space

1   A visiting company from the Far East is planning to use your performance space. They have asked for a space seven metres by five metres, blackout facilities, at least three 13 amp sockets, two separate entrances and space for a piece of free-standing scenery (a palace) which is three metres long and stands one metre and 25 centimetres away from a wall. You are keen to help this company of dancers, musicians and mime artists, who have a worldwide reputation. (They speak only a little English, however.) Make a ground plan showing how the space might be used and give any other information you consider useful.

2   You are taking a student company to the Edinburgh Festival to stage an improvised piece on the theme of 'The Power Struggle'. There will be twelve people in the company, and the director plans to include some dramatic fight work. The owners of the hall have sent you the rough ground plan opposite and a note pointing out that there is a new vinyl floor and the walls have been repainted; nothing must be used which will damage these surfaces. Safety regulations state that all

gangways must be one metre wide. Arrange the hall to allow a
reasonable performance area and to accommodate as large an
audience as possible, all of whom must be able to see in comfort and
safety.

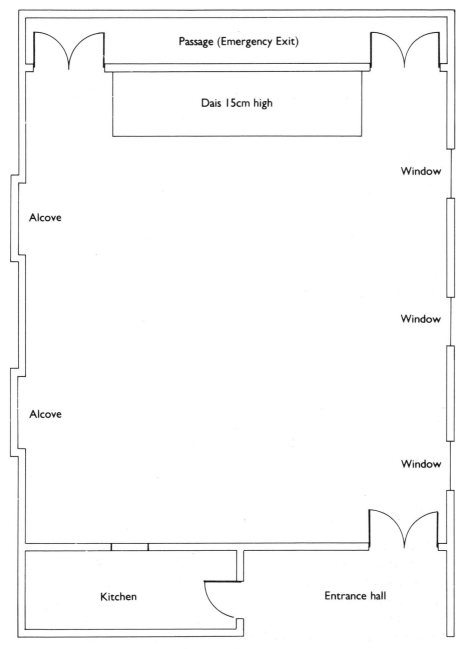

Diagram of a hall

AUDIENCE 2

Detail from 'Booth Stage 1608', by David Vinkeboons

> . . . the people began exceedingly to laugh when Tarlton first
> peeped out his head. Whereat the Justice . . . seeing he could
> not make them cease, he went with his staff and beat them
> round about unmercifully on their bare pates, in that they,
> being but farmers and poor country hinds, would presume to
> laugh at the Queen's men, and make no account of her cloth in
> his company.
>
> (from Thomas Nashe's *Pierce Penilesse*, 1592)

Tarlton was such a well-known comedian in Shakespeare's company of
actors that the Queen herself was supposed to have sent him out of the
room on one occasion because he made her laugh so uncontrollably.
But apart from the reference in this extract to the livery of one of the
Queen's men – her cloth – there is much here that could apply to an
audience today.

Are there comedians nowadays whose faces are so well-known that people will laugh as soon as they see them, as Tarlton's audience did? Do you know of audiences who will 'send up' a serious performance because they know the actor too well in real life? Can you think of occasions when the pretence of an actor's performance is mistaken for reality, or when the audience is actively subdued, perhaps quite aggressively, as both the Justice in the extract or the player in the picture is doing?

Before making too many assumptions about the nature of an audience or the material you may presume suitable for it, you might do well to do some more research. It is very easy to assume that senior citizens like music-hall, or that young children like fairy stories, but you need to see if there is any truth in these assumptions.

Very often, performers have material that they wish to perform for their own very good reasons. They will then announce the programme and hope for the right kind of audience to come along. Your circumstances may be different in that your performances may be presented for examination, or viewed in order to assess the work that has gone into them. It is a valuable exercise, however, to pay serious attention to what makes an audience, before considering how to present material in an appropriate way.

Group surveys

Surveys may sometimes be considered intrusive when they concern matters of taste, but a carefully worded questionnaire conducted in the neighbourhood might be revealing and helpful. Before embarking on a general survey that is aimed at assessing the full range of audience tastes, it might be of benefit to conduct a preliminary survey among fellow students about their critical appreciation of both recorded and live performances, their attitude towards actors and the theatre, and the reasons why they do or do not go to the theatre.

Assignments

1 A great deal can be achieved by watching the watchers. Try to visit a number of different performance spaces in your area. To avoid detracting from your own enjoyment of the performance, get to the theatre early and spend a few minutes observing the audience and the type of space and seating arrangement that they inhabit. How are

they dressed? What is their average age? Have they come singly or in groups? What is the nature of the entertainment? How are they expected to respond? Are they quiet? Is the auditorium dark? What do people do in the interval? Is there an interval? Can you observe any discussion of the performance? Do they seem satisfied? These are just some of the questions it would be valuable for you to think about: there are bound to be many more!

2 Study these caricatures of eighteenth century audiences. There is a great deal of information to be derived from them if you ask yourself the same questions about the audience in the pictures as you considered with reference to an audience of today.

Caricatures by Thomas Rowlandson

3 There are plans to convert a disused warehouse in your area into an arts centre. In order to use the space to the best advantage, a survey will be carried out to see what people want. You have been given responsibility for devising questions about future theatre use. Jot down some of the considerations you think most important when planning a theatre in this area and a list of about a dozen key questions for the survey.

4 The best way to find out about audience reaction is to devise a short programme for a very specific audience and perform it several times, taking particular note of the response. You may be able to talk to the audience afterwards about what they most enjoyed, whether they would like another performance and, if so, what they would like next time.

PERFORMANCE 3

A performance can take place anywhere and at any time, whenever there is an audience and a performer. There are times, however, when the two come together in special circumstances and have certain expectations of each other. On most of these occasions there exists an unwritten contract that the audience have come to be 'entertained'; to be 'taken out of themselves' or to celebrate some special event, and that the performer has come to fulfil those requirements.

The audience have chosen the performance to suit their needs, but the performer may have no idea what the audience wants, except that they have chosen to come to this particular show of their own free will and must therefore have some idea or expectation of what it is they are going to receive.

Unfortunately, performers are not often asked to think about the audience in advance; it is not seen as part of their craft to study audiences or to question what they might require from the performance. Nevertheless, it can be crucial to the style and level of the performance. To give one very simple example, what might an audience of young children require from a performance of a wicked uncle? The other actors need him to be realistically wicked in order to give them something to fight against; the children need a certain amount of excitement and they certainly need the uncle to be bad enough to justify his downfall. However, if the actor knows little or nothing about the reaction of young children to performances in the theatre, he may play a really bad man, so genuine in his nastiness that there will be real fear, rather than the thrill of simulated terror. In this case, more than a touch of over-acting, blustering or humour might be necessary to avoid real upset among the audience.

Audience expectations can be extremely limiting, especially to a well-known artist, whose audience come looking for exactly the same style, year after year, or to the student whose classmates may be used to an off-stage personality and may not be able to take a serious degree of characterisation. It is therefore important that anyone associated with theatre knows a good deal about audiences and that every student tackles the activities on pp. 27–29 before going on to consider working on a performance.

Generally speaking, the actual performance is the least creative part of the whole theatrical experience. Certainly there should be nothing radically different from the performance developed during rehearsals, except that the presence of an audience may cause subtle differences in presentation. The most creative and imaginative stage exists in the preparation by each member of the production team of the work that is to be performed.

Assignment

Your group is going to perform the following scene in one of the actor/audience arrangements you have already studied. Make very full notes to be given to the actors at the first rehearsal about how to perform in the space; about the audience you might expect; about the style of presentation and any problems the actors might anticipate.

Scene for performance in a number of different spaces

A. Would you care for a drink?
B. Would you?
C. Who? Me? Ah . . . No.
A. Is it too hot for you?
B. For me?
A. The other one. Is it too hot for the other one?
B. Shall I ask?
A. Yes, ask.
B. Is it too hot for you?
C. Hot? Ah . . . No. Too hot? . . . Not at all hot.
B. Oh . . . Oh dear. Maybe it's cold. Shall I feel?
A. No, don't feel.
C. Never feel . . . Feel nothing . . . Touch nothing . . . Touch nobody.

ACTING

It is often said that little or nothing can be achieved by an actor working alone, because drama is a group activity. This is obviously untrue, as may be seen from reading any one of the many interviews given by great performers. Probably 60 per cent of the final performance has been achieved as a result of private thought and study, not just by learning lines but through working long hours on the characterisation, and on the interpretation of the ideas expressed in the play from the viewpoint of that character.

Characterisation

1 Scripted material

The first reading of a play may take place in a group, but once the casting has been done, the actor needs to read the whole play several times in order to establish the style of the play and some kind of believable life-style for the character. It is never enough to go through the text, underline one's part, count the lines and then come to rehearsal to find out about characterisation, situation and style.

The approach should be the same, whatever the size of the part. An example is given here. It may be helpful to use the same method for every part you play.

Edna in *An Inspector Calls* by J. B. Priestley

This play was first produced in Moscow in 1945. It is set in the year 1912, and concerns the interruption, by 'An Inspector', of a dinner given by the Birling family to celebrate the engagement of Sheila Birling. By an elaborate theatrical contrivance, the 'Inspector' finally arouses some sense of the responsibility that each individual should bear towards the fate of others.

Edna is the maid. At the opening of the play she is clearing away the remains of the celebratory dinner and handing the decanter of port to the master of the house. She has two other entrances during the three acts of the play, to announce people who have arrived at the front door. Altogether she has six lines in the whole play, so why bother to include the character at all? What opportunities does it offer an actor? What preparation can possibly be done to make anything of such a miniscule part? The following may serve as an example of the kind of questions that an actor should ask before coming to rehearsals.

What function does the character serve in the structure of the play?

The presence of a maid shows the status of the family. At the time when the play was written, repertory theatres existed in most towns and this part was probably played by an assistant stage manager who would have been engaged, as part of a permanent company, to play small parts as well as to work backstage. This made it practicable to include someone on the payroll whose main functions as an actor was to tell the audience the name of those characters who were not part of the family.

What style of performance is called for?

The play has a serious message and the whole tone is sombre. There is not much in the way of light relief and, although Edna is not meant to be a comic character, her entrances do at least provide some added interest. She is an example of someone from a different class in a play where class, money and status are important, so she should be played as a down-to-earth woman, with a local accent. The play is set in 'Brumly', an imaginary North Midlands town which could be taken to be Birmingham.

What effect does the character have on the audience or on the other characters?

There is not a great deal of action in the play, but a great deal of dramatic tension; entrances are very important, and Edna's presence adds to the tension of such moments. The fact that she does not show 'the Inspector' of the title into the dining-room immediately, but keeps him waiting, says a great deal about his standing with the other characters.

How old is she?

There is no indication of how long she has been in service; however, since she does not need to be told what to do, we might assume that she is not very young.

What kind of person is she?

There is also a cook in the household, so as Edna is no longer a very young girl she is probably not well enough educated to rise above parlour maid and also possibly not very bright.

What does she look like?

The dress of a maid in the early 1900s is absolutely set, with different aprons and caps for evening and daytime. This is evening and a special occasion, so she will be wearing the uniform that is appropriate. It should also be borne in mind that such clothes are long, heavy and uncomfortable. A real maid would certainly have worn a corset, so the actor's movements should suggest a degree of uprightness. Appearances are important to the other characters so she should be tidy and well cared for.

What am I doing here?

This is a different sort of question because the answer has to be given by the actor on stage during every performance. Every character has both a long-term objective and a short-term one. Edna's long-term objective is to make the serving of this engagement dinner as much of an occasion as possible and then clear away and possibly wash up, in time to go to bed at a reasonably early hour. It follows, therefore, that her short-term objective is to get rid of the interruptions as quickly as possible. Near the end of the play, when the Inspector has gone, Edna has been told to wait up to make tea for the family. When she subsequently announces the return of one of the characters, it may be supposed that she is somewhat put out at all these comings and goings.

What are my feelings towards the other characters?

Again, this is something that needs to be thought about on stage as well as beforehand. In the play, Edna has no obviously expressed attitudes, except towards the Inspector, but, since every actor needs to supply these for herself, it is reasonable to imagine that she finds Mr Birling rather pretentious, but is anxious to please Mrs Birling; that she favours Sheila's engagement and despises Eric for his drinking problem.

Assignment

Take one of the minor characters from a play by Shakespeare, for example the porter in *Macbeth*, or the clown in *Antony and Cleopatra*. Apply the same process as was applied to Edna in *An Inspector Calls*, but instead of playing the scene or scenes in which the character appears, narrate the story, in role, of your involvement in the great events surrounding you. The character will not know the whole story but can only guess at the reasons for what is going on and observe only what happens in his or her presence.

An Edwardian maid in evening uniform

2   Devised or improvised material

When it comes to performing a devised or improvised piece, the same questions have to be asked, but in this case the answers will depend not on reading the text but on the way the material has been built up during rehearsals. Such matters as the style of performance, the relevance of the character to the theme and structure of the piece may have been established early on, but there is a danger that during the process of structuring the whole, the characters may not have been sufficiently developed: they may have become mouthpieces for the ideas expressed in the piece, or, having been the mainspring of the work throughout the improvisation, have now become overdrawn to the point of becoming stereotypes.

To restore the balance, the actor needs to have the same responsibility towards the ultimate performance as if the play had been scripted from the beginning. It may seem selfish, but during the performance the actor's concentration should be on the communication of the character and that character's situation, and not on the structuring of the play.

Building up a character from scratch allows for greater choice. It is good practice to observe other people and to take certain characteristics from a study of the way they move, speak and approach others. Sometimes just one simple gesture or way of speaking can become the keynote for a whole character. Actors in training often spend a considerable time making a special study of one animal in a zoo. This may not be practicable for you, but it is perfectly possible to go to the relevant place to study character: a meeting, a street market, a shopping centre, on buses and trains and at stations. Anywhere where people congregate can form a useful 'zoo' of people to study.

Assignments

1 Whenever appropriate, try representing a character you have studied. This can be done deliberately for practice, in which case each member of the group may show their character studies and answer questions, either in role or as a third person, about the chosen character. The other way to bring previously studied characters into improvised work is to introduce them into any appropriate situations as part of a stock of characters which you have prepared. This is a technique that is often used by those comedians who play sketches. They keep a supply of characters to use in different situations. They are usually broadly based, even caricatured, and all of them are instantly recognisable. A serious actor will want to avoid repeating the characters, as often as a comedian usually does, simply to avoid that instant recognition and to achieve a degree of subtlety.

2 Write or record and rehearse, and finally perform a monologue, based on your observation of a character in the 'human zoo' situation. Although you will have invented the circumstances of this character's

life, try to make it as real as possible. It would be most helpful if your audience could comment on how well they feel they know the character after your performance.

Technique

Much of an actor's technique is a matter of physical training. It is extremely important to practise relaxation, so that it becomes something that you can feel in yourself, standing or sitting. It is also necessary to work at voice exercises, breathing and posture. Some of this can be done without anyone else being aware that you are, for example, exercising breathing while you are walking, or exercising relaxation sitting on a bus, but sometimes actors are embarrassed at doing voice exercises or going through a part aloud. In such cases, it is worthwhile working with someone else, sharing practice time and helping each other by hearing lines and so on. Time spent in practice can establish a lifetime's routine of useful exercise.

There are many other techniques which can be studied alone, such as make-up, facial expression, crying, laughing, pitch and phrasing. An actor needs to spend just as much thinking and practice time as any instrumentalist, singer or dancer.

Group work

Much of the work in any acting workshop will be spent in the formation of the group itself. There are many games and exercises designed to increase group awareness and sensitivity, but in the end it is the final product that will bring the group together. Sometimes playing games can be merely a way of postponing the major activity, and, apart from warm-up exercises, most of the group's preparation time needs to be planned with a clear objective.

There are two distinct phases of work which should concern the members of the group; the first is discussion and planning and the other is experiment. It is always useful to keep a diary, and to record and analyse progress, both from an individual point of view and from the point of the shaping of the work in hand. This record, if it is honest, will be very helpful in showing how to conduct group work in successive sessions.

Discussion and planning

Discussion is a very necessary part of the group's activity, but also a very difficult process to handle. In the business world, people can spend a great deal of time on learning how to conduct good discussion sessions. It is always useful to find an objective that can be clearly stated, such as a planning session or a review of progress, and then to set a time limit. It may be helpful to record in the diary the time spent in discussion, how many people participated, whether there was a clear outcome, and whether it was helpful to everyone or useful in establishing a single idea.

Planning may be the most important aspect of discussion in a group-devised piece, but revision and assessment of achievement at various stages of the work also take a great deal of skill. In many cases it may be more productive to leave assessment to the beginning of the next session so that it can lead straight into further work rather than to try to catch the red-hot mood of creativity immediately it has happened. Recollection in tranquillity can often be very helpful, but there also needs to be time at the end of each session for reflection. This involves individuals thinking back over the session and making a few notes, or just brooding for a moment or two about what has been achieved and where there were blocks or unsatisfactory moments in the creative process.

Experiment

The term experiment in the theatrical sense covers both rehearsal and any sequence of improvisation or exercise that leads to a final product. When it is well handled it can be the most creative part of the performance process. Most actors enjoy creating and rehearsing the final shape of a production more than performing in a long run, since there is always something new to discover and further experiments to make in the interpretation of a play or a devised piece.

By working as part of a creative group, actors learn to become sensitive to the needs of others and how to promote the shaping of the piece to be performed. There is a fine balance to be learned between taking the initiative in ideas and performance and acquiring the ability to listen constructively to what other people have to say. Reflecting on your own ability to be part of a team is something that needs to be taken seriously. To ensure that the creative period is enjoyable, everyone taking part needs to be fully aware of the whole process. As with discussion, there is a great deal to be gained from keeping a diary and recording what has been achieved. There have been a number of published diaries or accounts of rehearsals which might give you some ideas before starting on your own record.

Spend the time when you are not rehearsing in watching other people work, and analyse and record the results. Look at the balance of repetition versus improvisation. Note who initiates the improvisation and whether it is directly related to the understanding of the piece or whether it contributes in other ways. Record how often something is repeated and what is achieved. It is often surprising how much time can be devoted to work on a few lines of text. Keep a tally of the time spent on consolidating a passage or scene. Consider to what extent any of the methods used during the session are productive or the cause of friction. Look also for the amount of input from either the director or individual actors in your own and other people's scenes. As well as noting whether you found the input helpful, suggest other approaches which could also be appropriate.

As a student of Theatre Arts, you should be constantly stockpiling experience and technique for the future, and learning from watching others working is one of the best experiences you can have.

Assignments

1 It is not often possible to watch professional theatre companies at work, but if such opportunities arise, make the most of them. It is often acceptable, however, to sit in on rehearsals of other performance arts in your own place of work. Take the opportunity of studying how dancers or musicians approach group work and most particularly the role of the director or teacher in those sessions.

2 Think over what discoveries you have made about the character you are playing, as a result of working with others in the group, and to what extent your original characterisation has changed and developed. Use the term 'discovery' as part of your approach to a play. What other 'discoveries' have you made with reference to the theme, style or structure of the piece as a result of group work? Devise an exercise or improvisation that relates directly to some aspect of the piece you are studying. Try it out and judge its merits by what discoveries it brings about for yourself or others.

39

DIRECTING

The ultimate objective of a director must be to be part of a whole production team and to act as initiator and co-ordinator of the work of the team that includes all design and technical departments. To that extent, it is not possible to carry out a full study of this aspect of Theatre Arts until much later in the course. However, it is important to keep thinking about directing, because in so doing you will be actively considering the interpretation of a theatre piece as it affects the work of the whole team. This section, therefore, will be concerned with the directing of actors and the interpretation of text from the actor's point of view.

Preparation

The first meeting with a group one is about to direct is a very nervous occasion. So much depends on the actors' willingness to collaborate to make a success of the work in hand, and this in turn, depends upon the director's approach.

Ask yourself what right you have to direct actors in the piece, and then provide yourself with an answer based on the work you have already done before you think of meeting the cast. Doing a substantial amount of homework on the text will give you a true sense of security and the necessary background to enthuse the actors.

Your choice of text will have been based on the opportunities it offers. Try to set out in writing what the piece has to say, what its likely appeal to an audience might be and what interests you about the characters and the style of writing.

Make sure that you have read the whole play if you are doing an extract, since the interpretation of a single scene must fit into the meaning of the whole, especially as far as characterisation is concerned. Read the scene so thoroughly that every line makes sense and so you understand the implications in every line. There is little to be gained by choosing anything but the best: a really well written scene will have depths of understanding that will provide you with many opportunities for discovery during rehearsals, whereas a poorly written sketch or trivial scene has very little to work on and therefore is actually more difficult to rehearse successfully.

Stage directions also need to be read carefully. There is no need to reproduce every move or placing of scenery, but there are varying degrees of usefulness and it is often unwise to disregard them without careful thought. Try to visualise the implication of moves, gestures or outside influences such as the weather, noises off, or lighting effects since they may well contribute to the meaning of the play.

Some directors plan the staging of a piece very carefully beforehand, using models or stage plans sketched on blank pages interleaved into the script, with every move carefully written down, whereas others have only a general idea of the placing of the characters. Whichever method you choose, it should be a matter of deliberate choice based on the time available for rehearsals, the nature of the script and knowing how you want the actors to respond – not because of insufficient preparation.

The most important consideration of all is the style of presentation that the play requires. To work against the style of a piece can sometimes produce an interesting performance, but it has to be done knowingly. Mistakes in establishing the style of presentation are usually disastrous. Ask yourself basic questions such as, is this meant to be played realistically? If it is comedy, is it verbal or visual comedy? Is the audience involved directly? Is there an overall mood to the play?

Having read the piece in detail, you will then have to make up a special script with space for the notes you have made or will make in rehearsal. It will certainly be important to decide on how to arrange the acting area and the focus of the audience's attention. It may be necessary to mark in some important moves or positions so that the audience can easily focus on the central action or character at key moments. There is an example overleaf of how a page of script might look:

sweep *Rod*

Sag *flower*

Sarah

Knocker

Knocker cart

Knocker

① Bell live

② Off stage R. at back

③ Knocker U.S.L.   swe-e-ep very high voice

④ taps on steps L.

⑤ Behind audience

⑥ Run up steps. C. knocks

⑦ knocks high rostrum

⑧ Sag opens window has rag curlers and a shawl. Others coming on a) Man with handcart b) flower seller c) Crier. All mocking Sagamour.

⑨ knocker curtsies

⑩ Warm voice to call Sarah (who lives below sagamour).

⑪ Music cue and beginning of song

Crier A street in the City of London in the early Eighteenth Century. It is not long after Dawn. A clock strikes seven. ① *In the distance a sweep-boy calls out from* ② *the top of a chimney 'Sweep, sweep!'* ③ *KNOCKER, a small, scruffy urchin with a long stick, runs along the street and taps on a few windows with it.*

SWEEP. Sweep! Chimney sweep!

④ KNOCKER. Seven o'clock, Mister Bull!

⑤ CRIER. Seven o'clock and all's well.

⑥ KNOCKER. Seven o'clock Mistress Rodd; it's gone seven. ⑦ Seven o'clock M'lady Saggy-bags!

⑧ MRS SAGAMOUR. It's one minute past, and don't you call me names!

KNOCKER. D'you wan't a call or don't you, Mistress Saggy-bags ⑨ . . . me lady? ⑩ Seven o'clock Sarah.

MRS SAGAMOUR. Impudence! ⑪ I pays you don't I?

CRIER. Seven o'clock and all's well.

Director's script: a page from Moll Flanders

Assignments

1 Interpreting the author's instructions

Study the following introduction to a play in which the author gives a
great deal of information. Draw up a rough stage plan that follows
those instructions. In what style would you direct the actors to play,
based only on the information given here?

An extract from *Con*, Act One, Scene One

> *Early morning, misty and cold. You can see right through* PATRICK
> MULVANNEY*'s boat shed to the landing stage beyond, since both sets of
> double doors are open. In the shed is a stone-built copper with a
> wooden lid, a grindstone, herring boxes, rope, a curragh hung on the
> roof timbers, barrels, bowls and general clutter, but it's very clean, so
> you'd know where to find things. There is a door, up some stone steps
> that leads into the house, and beyond the sea wall are some more steps
> [unseen] that lead to the Atlantic, rolling far below, oily and quiet in
> the mist. A seagull is fussing quietly over something he lost out at sea,
> a few hens brood gently, no one about.*
>
> > *Suddenly there's the most appalling, long-drawn-out, squealing cry
> > that ends abruptly. It is followed by thumps and crashes in the house
> > and the cries of startled gulls and hens. A terrible row!*
>
> *Several women come in, muffled and shawled against the cold.*

EVELEEN.   Blessed Jesus! That was his death-cry, surely.

NAN.   A great and terrible cry.

EVELEEN.   It should be a fine, fat fellow sings like that and his throat
cut.

> [*Carmel enters, crying loudly.*]

UNA.   Oh you, Carmel Hickey, what on earth are you crying for?

CARMEL.   It only seems a day ago that I carried him in my arms, and
him just a little, runty fella, with the small, blue eyes and the
skin on him like soft, pink silk.

SIOBHAN [*snivelling*].   And the trusting way he had of looking at you!

CARMEL [*still crying*].   And the little fair hairs sticking out of his ears!

UNA.   It's like murdering a baby! [*she begins to howl*]

43

NAN. Ah, now, hold your tongues the lot of you. There's work to be done here, before his precious life's blood runs to waste on the dry rocks below. [*she adds to the screeching by sharpening a butcher's knife on the grindstone*] Pour me some water here. Come on!

CARMEL. I fed him myself with the little spuds too small for the pot.

SIOBHAN. And the first day's milk, from the goat gave birth to a billy-kid.

NAN. Fetch in the salt, will you? [*no one does*]

SIOBHAN [*keening*]. Poor Lazarus.

CARMEL and UNA [*keening*]. Ah, Lazarus, he's gone.

EVELEEN [*on her knees, stoking and blowing the fire under the copper*]. God rest him and all of his name that went before. He fed on the crumbs that fell from the rich man's table, and now, by the Grace of God, he'll see us through the winter.

NAN. SALT! [*she tests the knife blade on her thumb*]

[*The house door opens and* SHELAGH *appears at the top of the steps. She wears a huge hessian apron drenched in fresh blood and carries a cleaver in her hand.*]

EVELEEN. Bloody Mary!

[*The girls gasp and cross themselves.*]

2 Interpreting mood without instruction

When authors give no instruction, the concentration is usually on language and mood. How would you divide up the following chorus to give a number of distinct characters? Photocopy and mark the script accordingly.

A Chorus from *The Fall of Troy* to be spoken by a group

[*It is the hour before dawn. Outside the city of Argos a group of women assemble.*]

WOMEN. Did you hear something? I was asleep. I had this dream. There was a noise. I don't remember. Someone cried out. Perhaps a hyena. Perhaps a hunted animal in a snare. A terrible dream. Darkness and no stars. I dreamed of blood. The moon full of blood and no stars. Vultures screamed all night. Was it a dream? Fires in the sky. The cries of dying animals. Fear in the night. Waking and walking in the dark. What does it mean?

[CLYTEMNESTRA *enters*]

WOMEN. Is something wrong? We heard noises in the night. Clytemnestra, what has happened? Why this sacrificial fire? There are signs. Lights in the sky. Moving lights. Won't you tell us? Have you news?

Rehearsals

Actors do not always get a great deal from a first reading. Even experienced actors find that reading through the play or scene can be depressing to all concerned, although the quickest and easiest way of going through the text may be to read it together. This certainly avoids the problems caused by actors reading the script first at home and arriving with fixed ideas about the size of their part or the interpretation of the character before they are ready to do any private study. However, it may be preferable to introduce the style, themes and situation and even the characters in a play by working an exercise or improvisation first.

Script reading can be split up into short sections, each of which is prepared through improvisation or even through games. For example, a play which is about power could be introduced very quickly by playing some version of King of the Castle or through Master and Slave games. Then the idea of sitting down to read a scene illustrating the idea in theatrical terms becomes less threatening.

Casting through reading is never very satisfactory. Role-play and improvisation are more useful in determining casting. If the group is used to working together it may be possible to choose the play to suit the actors while avoiding the cruder elements of type-casting. If the work is intended for workshop use and not for public performance, where copyright may be involved, a great deal may be gained by changing some roles from young to old or from men to women.

Always try to plan your approach to suit the objective for each rehearsal. Being aware of the difficulties that will certainly occur during rehearsals and suggesting a new approach or asking the actors for suggestions as to how to improvise a way round a problem may lead to new discoveries.

As with acting, the best way to learn about conducting rehearsals is to watch others at work and then to find the method that suits you and the play best.

Assignments

I   As an exercise in interpretation, try directing the following scene in two different ways, first playing the characters as women and then playing them as men. What do they, and you, find out about potential interpretations of text by these changes?

An extract from *Waiting for Godot*, by Samuel Beckett, Act One

POZZO.   Turn! [LUCKY *turns. To* VLADIMIR *and* ESTRAGON, *affably.*] Gentlemen, I am happy to have met you. [*Before their incredulous expression.*] Yes, yes, sincerely happy. [*He jerks the rope.*] Closer! [LUCKY *advances.*] Stop! [LUCKY *stops.*] Yes, the road seems long when one journeys all alone for . . . [*he consults his watch*] . . . yes . . . [*he calculates*] . . . yes, six hours, that's right, six hours on end, and never a soul in sight. [*To* LUCKY.] Coat! [LUCKY *puts down the bag, advances, gives the coat, goes back to his place, takes up the bag.*] Hold that! [POZZO *holds out the whip.* LUCKY *advances and, both his hands being occupied, takes the whip in his mouth, then goes back to his place.* POZZO *begins to put on his coat, stops.*] Coat! [LUCKY *puts down bag, basket and stool, advances, helps* POZZO *on with his coat, goes back to his place and takes up bag, basket and stool.*] Touch of autumn in the air this evening. [POZZO *finishes buttoning his coat, stoops, inspects himself, straightens up.*] Whip! [LUCKY *advances, stoops,* POZZO *snatches the whip from his mouth,* LUCKY *goes back to his place.*] Yes, gentlemen, I cannot go for long without the society of my likes [*he puts on his glasses and looks at the two likes*] even when the likeness is an imperfect one. [*He takes off his glasses.*] Stool! [LUCKY *puts down bag and basket, advances, opens stool, puts it down, goes back to his place, takes up bag and basket.*] Closer! [LUCKY *puts down bag and basket, advances, moves stool, goes back to his place, takes up bag and basket.* POZZO *sits down, places the butt of his whip against* LUCKY'S *chest and pushes.*] Back! [LUCKY *takes a step back.*] Further! [LUCKY *takes another step back.*] Stop! [LUCKY *stops. To* VLADIMIR *and* ESTRAGON.] That is why, with your permission, I propose to dally with you a moment, before I venture any further. Basket! [LUCKY *advances, gives the basket, goes back to his place.*] The fresh air stimulates the jaded appetite. [*He opens the basket, takes out a piece of chicken and a bottle of wine.*] Basket! [LUCKY *advances, picks up the basket, goes back to his place.*] Further! [LUCKY *takes a step back.*] He stinks. Happy days!

He drinks from the bottle, puts it down and begins to eat. Silence. VLADIMIR *and* ESTRAGON, *cautiously at first, then more boldly, begin to circle about* LUCKY, *inspecting him up and down.* POZZO *eats his chicken voraciously, throwing away the bones after having sucked them.* LUCKY *sags slowly, until bag and basket touch the ground, then straightens up with a start and begins to sag again. Rhythm of one sleeping on his feet.*

ESTRAGON.   What ails him?

VLADIMIR.   He looks tired.

ESTRAGON.   Why doesn't he put down his bags?

VLADIMIR.   How do I know? [*They close in on him.*] Careful!

ESTRAGON.   Say something to him.

VLADIMIR.   Look!

ESTRAGON.   What?

VLADIMIR [*pointing*].   His neck!

ESTRAGON [*looking at his neck*].   I see nothing.

VLADIMIR.   Here.

[ESTRAGON *goes over beside* VLADIMIR.]

ESTRAGON.   Oh I say.

VLADIMIR.   A running sore!

ESTRAGON.   It's the rope.

VLADIMIR.   It's the rubbing.

ESTRAGON.   It's inevitable.

VLADIMIR.   It's the knot.

ESTRAGON.   It's the chafing.

[*They resume their inspection, dwell on the face.*]

VLADIMIR [*grudgingly*].   He's not bad looking.

ESTRAGON [*shrugging his shoulders, wry face*].   Would you say so?

2 Devise an improvisation that will establish the situation of the villagers in the following scene; then read the scene together, standing or walking about, rather than sitting down. Discuss the effect of the improvisation on the reading.

An extract from *Brand* by Henrik Ibsen, Act Two, Scene One (edited version)

A small, but desperate crowd on the quay-side is scrambling for the food being rationed out by a harassed official.

OFFICIAL [*catching sight of* BRAND].   Welcome stranger! No doubt you've heard about the floods and famine. All contributions thankfully received. We've spent the little we could raise. Five loaves and three small fishes leave but little over nowadays.

BRAND.   Five or five thousand in any other name but God's is valueless.

OFFICIAL.   I didn't ask for speeches; words are no better than stones to the starving.

PEOPLE.   He rejects us!

OFFICIAL.   He's mocking us for helping you.

A WOMAN.   Look, a squall has got up as if it heard what he said and was angry!

ANOTHER.   God will not be mocked.

BRAND.   Your God will not give you miracles.

CROWD.   Look at the sky! It's all because of him! Get him down, heartless brute! Stone him!

A WOMAN [*running in wildly*].   Help me! Get help, in Christ's name!

OFFICIAL.   What? What is it?

WOMAN.   The worst you can imagine this side of hell!

OFFICIAL.   What is it? Speak!

WOMAN.   I can't. Find me a priest.

OFFICIAL.   We have no priest here.

WOMAN.   Then he's lost!

BRAND.   A priest may not be far away.

WOMAN [*clutching his arm*].   Then let him come, quickly.

BRAND.   Tell me your need and I will come.

WOMAN.   Three starving children . . . The food all gone . . . Oh, say he isn't damned!

BRAND.   Speak first.

WOMAN.   Famine had dried my milk. Man never came to our aid. God never smiled. The baby fought with death . . . He couldn't bear it . . . He killed . . .

CROWD.   Killed . . . His own child?

WOMAN.   Then, struck dumb with remorse he turned on himself . . . You must save his soul . . . He cannot live and he dare not die. He lies, cradling the child's body and shrieking to all the Powers of Darkness. Oh, come and save him.

BRAND.   Yes. Here is need! A boat . . . Get me over there!

CROWD.   What! In this storm. No-one would dare! There's a path leads round the fiord.

WOMAN.   No, no! I came that way, but the bridge went just after I had crossed.

BRAND.   Unmoor a boat!

CROWD.   Look at the sea on the rocks! The whole fiord is seething!

49

Look at that gust off the cliffs. With such a sea you'll never make it.

BRAND.   When there's a dying man's soul to save, who waits on wind and water? [*he goes to the boat and loosens the sail*] Will you risk the boat?

BOAT OWNER.   Yes, but . . .

BRAND.   Good, now who will risk their life? [*the crowd demurs loudly with various reasons*] Your God helps no one; but my God is with me now, on board this boat. One brave man to help bale will do. You gave to life, now, who will give himself to death?

CROWD.   Do not ask that! Come back to land. You're tempting the wrath of God. Look, the storm is rising. The rope's broken . . .

AGNES.   I will come with you. [*she jumps into the boat*]

EINAR.   Agnes!

CROWD.   Stop! Turn back! Christ save her!

BRAND.   Which way?

WOMAN.   Right over the fiord, behind the black rock on that headland.

EINAR.   Think what you are doing! Think of your mother left childless!

CROWD.   He's cleared the point. No! Yes, look, it lies there. A gust has caught it. His hat's blown away. His hair is streaming out, black as a raven's wing in the wild air. The fiord is boiling. I heard a scream piercing through the storm! It came from the mountain. There stands Gerd, laughing and hooting after them. Aye, hoot and shriek you ugly troll! God is shielding and watching over that man's soul. I'll go in worse wind and storm next time, without a word, as long as he was aboard. Who was he?

EINAR.   A priest.

STAGE MANAGEMENT

The chief requirement of any good stage manager is the one most difficult to fulfil. Stage managers are both the right hand of the director *and* the essential link between all the different departments of the production team. This means that very often a stage manager is expected to be in two places at once. For this reason there are usually several people in a stage management team, but for the purposes of learning the skills involved, the job will be treated here as the responsibility of one person. (The shortened form of the title – SM – will also be used.)

From the beginning of the technical rehearsals through to the end of the last performance, and beyond, the SM is in sole charge of the stage. For centuries the SM had sole responsibility for the conduct of rehearsals and performances, since it was not considered necessary for anyone other than the actors to interpret a play. The position of producer or director is a twentieth century invention but the SM is still the person who 'holds the book' and who controls the entire performance in the theatre. Because of this controlling function, an SM needs to be a calming and stable presence throughout the excitable business of putting on a play. In the professional theatre and in television, having been an SM is the recommended pathway towards being a director, since stage managers often take rehearsals and rehearse understudies.

Preparation

If a text is being used, there is a great deal of creative study to be done before rehearsals begin. If the show is to be devised during rehearsals, then much of the thinking is the same, but there will be less information to go on. Before the production team can begin work, there will have to be a production meeting, and before the production meeting the stage manager will need the answers to certain questions. Some of these answers will come from the director, but there are many directors who will not have given any thought to such matters until they are raised by the SM. There are some questions to which the answer must be sought out, deduced from the script, or left to a later stage in rehearsals.

Some of the areas that you, as SM, will need to find out about are:

- If there is more than one location in the piece, will there be changes of set?

- Are there any parts that will be played by the same actor (doubled)?

- Is there to be live music? Does permission have to be obtained to use it?

- Is the play under copyright? Has permission been obtained for public performance? Are royalties payable?

- Are there any weapons or 'bangs', and is a firearms certificate needed?

- Are there any special effects that need to be made or hired?

- Are there to be any special arrangements of the stage or auditorium? Do these conform to the fire and safety regulations? Are there to be any naked lights on stage?

You will also need to look through the play carefully, especially at the stage directions, for any mention of 'props', either hand properties such as cigarette lighters or fans, or stage properties such as food on the table or a stagecoach and three white horses. Do these things have to be made, hired or borrowed? They will certainly have to be listed and checked with the director to make sure that they are essential to the production. It is also as well to check through all obvious lighting and sound effects and make a note of them, although you will be able to find out about most of them during rehearsals.

This making and checking of lists sounds tedious, but it is an interesting way to read a play and there is nothing so disheartening to a member of the stage crew than to spend a deal of energy in making or getting something which is not needed in the final production. Inevitable changes will be made and props will be added to the list, but it is as well to be thoroughly prepared before the first rehearsal.

It is not too soon to begin compiling a resource book of useful addresses, such as a list of professional hire firms for electrical and other specialist equipment, and local shopkeepers or residents who might lend equipment in return for a mention in the programme. Records will have to be kept, too, of everything borrowed, hired or bought so that items can be returned quickly.

Rehearsals

There will need to be two versions of 'the book', or stage manager's copy of the play. During rehearsals you will need one copy, interleaved with blank pages on which to note all the stage moves and pieces of action happening on or off stage. Before the technical rehearsal you will also have to mark all the cues for the lighting and sound operators. For this purpose you may need to make a second, fresh copy without all the rehearsal notes, but with every warning and cue carefully numbered and marked in colour. This copy will remain in the SM corner of the stage during performances. An example is shown on page 54. With such an exact record of the running of the performance always in place, the show can still go on, in spite of last minute non-arrivals of stage crew or even of the absence of the SM herself.

The SM is responsible for calling rehearsals, for setting out rehearsal space, marking out the acting area on the floor, if possible, providing substitute props to rehearse with, and prompting or 'reading in' parts, as well as recording changes in moves or significant pauses. It is obvious that by the end of the rehearsal period the SM will know the play better than anyone else. This does not mean, however, that anything can be left to memory; during performances the SM will be using her copy of the play to cue everyone backstage, more or less by numbers.

In the case of a devised piece, there will have to be a scenario, if not a complete script, before there can be any degree of stage management. A series of cues will have to be worked out with the actors if the piece is improvised and there is no exact script.

Assignments

1 The best, if not the only way, to learn how to run a performance is to act as assistant to an SM. Sitting in on rehearsals or assisting with lighting, sound or workshop responsibilities are all part of the practical training.

2 Photocopy and mark the scene on page 55 with all the proper warnings and cues. Notice that some of the cues are marked 'live' and you will have to imagine where to place each effect and how to cue it. All the information and help you need can be found in the sample given on page 54.

An example of how a page from an SM copy might look

	LX WARN LX Q 5 33,34,35	FX WARN FX Q'S 14,15 WARN OP Q2 (DOOR)
Gareth stays slumped in his chair in the last glimmerings of daylight from the tiny window. The wind whistles gently in the chimney, but suddenly a gust, stronger than the others, blows open the cottage door. Gareth jumps up and closes it, locking and bolting it in a sudden fury of activity. The wind dies to a moan. Noticing for the first time how late it has become, he switches on the standard lamp, which casts a small circle of light behind the heavy, old sofa. Crossing to the window he pulls the curtains and shuts out the last of the setting sun. He puts a couple of logs on the fire and pokes it until it sparks and flickers and then burns up with a rosy glow that illuminates the shabby room.	GO LX Q33 (GREEN) (VISUAL AS G SWIT- CHES LAMP) GO LX Q 34 (GREEN) (VISUAL AS CURTAINS CLOSE) GO LX Q 35 (VISUAL) (GREEN) (FLICKER, THEN BRING UP)	GO FX 14 (GUST) (GREEN) GO OP Q2 (DOOR) (GREEN) GO FX 15 (VISUAL) (GREEN) (AS DOOR CLOSES)

Scene for assignment 2

Jane switches off the office lights and leaves, closing and locking the door. There is a moment's silence and then, through the glass of the door, a wavering torchlight can be seen. A much magnified scratching sound is heard, as the intruder picks the lock. A woman wearing a dark tracksuit, enters, picking out the desk and filing cabinet with her torch, which she then places so that it creates a small circle of light.

She picks the filing cabinet lock and, riffling through the files, chooses one; then picking up the torch, she brings it over to the desk. Switching out the torch, she bends down the desk-lamp and turns it on. Producing a small camera from her pocket, she proceeds to photograph page after page of the file.

After a second or two, footsteps are heard plodding up the stairs [live sound], and the intruder switches off the desk-lamp.

CARETAKER. I'm sure I saw a light.

OFFICER. Could have been a reflection from the street. But we'll just take a look round to be sure. Have you got the key?

The lock is opened [this time it is a live sound] and the lights are switched on, illuminating the whole office. There is nothing unusual to be seen, no intruder, no open file, no unlocked filing cabinet.

T013981

3 The following scene from an eighteenth century comedy is to be staged as authentically as possible. Write a list of the questions you might need to ask the director. (Provide answers from the text, where possible.)

An extract from *The Critic, or A Tragedy Rehearsed* by R. B. Sheridan

PUFF.   – Now then for my magnificence! – my battle! – my noise! – and my procession! – You are all ready?

UND. PROMPT [*Within.*].   Yes, sir.

PUFF.   Is the Thames dressed?

[*Enter* THAMES *with two* ATTENDANTS.]

THAMES.   Here I am, sir.

PUFF.   Very well indeed! – See, gentlemen, there's a river for you! – This is blending a little of the masque with my tragedy – a new fancy, you know – and very useful in my case; for as there must be a procession, I suppose Thames, and all his tributary rivers, to compliment Britannia with a fête in honour of the victory.

SNEER.   But pray, who are these gentlemen in green with him?

PUFF.   Those? – those are his banks.

SNEER.   His banks?

PUFF.   Yes, one crowned with alders, and the other with a villa! – you take the allusions? – But hey! what the plague! – you have got both your banks on one side. – Here, sir, come round. – Ever while you live, Thames, go between your banks. – [*Bell rings.*] There, so! now for't! – Stand aside, my dear friends! – Away, Thames!

[*Exit* THAMES *between his banks.*]

[*Flourish of drums, trumpets, cannon, &c., &c. Scene changes to the sea – the fleets engage – the music plays 'Britons, strike home.' – Spanish fleet destroyed by fire-ships, &c. – English fleet advances – music plays 'Rule Britannia.' – The procession of all the English rivers, and their tributaries, with their emblems, &c., begins with*

*Handel's water music, ends with a chorus to the march in Judas
Maccabaeus. – During this scene,* PUFF *directs and applauds
everything – then –*]

PUFF.   Well, pretty well – but not quite perfect. So, ladies and
gentlemen, if you please, we'll rehearse this piece again
to-morrow.

[*Curtain drops.*]

THE END

Scene from The Critic *by Sheridan*

Lighting a play means lighting the actors. Only when you can be sure that the audience can see the actors' expressions clearly and without dazzle can you move on to lighting the set.

The effect of lighting from below

The effect of lighting from above

The effect of lighting from behind

The effect of lighting from the side

The effect of lighting from in front

The effect of lighting from above and in front

There are certain problems associated with lighting actors, chief of which is the fact that they are not usually free to come to a lighting session because of the pressures of rehearsal. In such cases it is important that the electrical department (LX) goes to see at least one full run-through or rehearsal of the play.

By the time the play is ready to run through, the lumieres or stage lanterns may have been rigged above the acting area, but it is obviously far better for the LX to see for themselves the actors' faces and the range of precise actions that have to be lit, than to rely on the director's notes or lighting plan. It is also essential for the LX to attend the production meeting before rehearsals begin, to find out from the SM whether there are any special requirements, and also to have a special planning session with the director.

LX operators and designers should know their equipment well before they come to light a play. For the sake of Health and Safety requirements, for the effective maintenance of expensive lumieres and to ensure the quickest and best ways of operating the lighting controls, it is absolutely essential that anyone handling theatre lighting knows exactly what they are doing. It would not be safe to learn this from a book; it must be taught on the equipment itself.

Preparation

Having read the play, seen the rehearsal and the director's rough lighting plan, lighting the play can begin.

The first matter to consider is the arrangement of the audience; lighting a play from the front is much easier than lighting a play in the round, and lighting a high ceilinged hall is simpler than lighting the average drama studio, but whatever the problems the lighting must be arranged in such a way that no one in the audience is blinded or is on the dark side of the actors. At the same time, every acting area must be well covered and every vantage point must be reached from at least two angles.

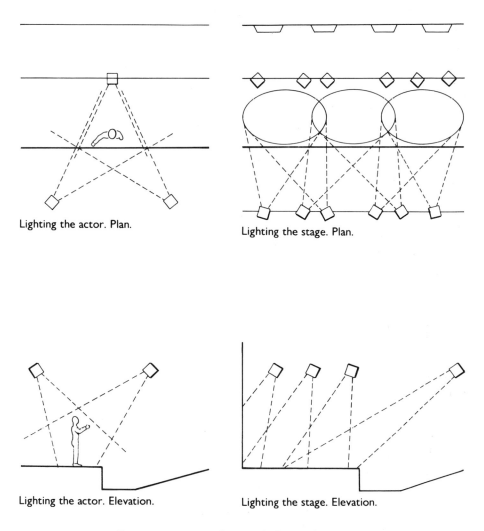

Lighting the actor. Plan.

Lighting the stage. Plan.

Lighting the actor. Elevation.

Lighting the stage. Elevation.

Proscenium or end stage lighting diagrams

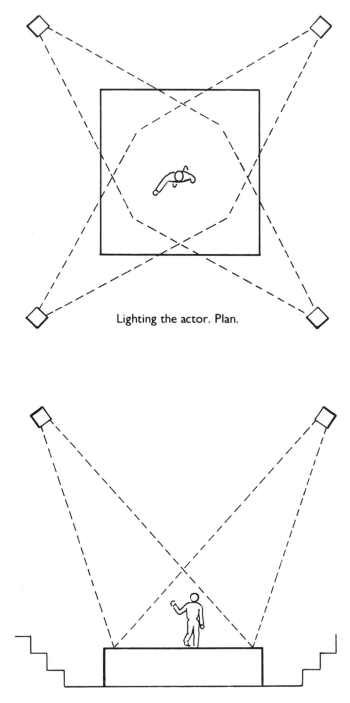

Lighting the actor. Plan.

Lighting the actor. Elevation.

In the round or open stage lighting diagrams

Discussing the production with the director is the first step. Careful and experienced directors will have a clear idea of what it is they want from the lighting, but LX will still have many questions to ask. There may well be differences in style between the written text and the production, and special emphasis on the mood of certain scenes may be needed. A number of different locations, scene changes or musical numbers may also be involved which would suggest very radical lighting changes, perhaps even requiring replugging or switching during the show.

From a reading of the play you will have noticed any *actual* lighting cues, such as where someone carries a candle across the stage or turns on a lamp, but there may be other effects, or moments where there needs to be a special focus on one actor, which are not evident from either the reading or the rehearsal, and which you will need to check with the director.

Colour and mood are most important when it comes to lighting the set and costumes. It can be effective, but difficult and wasteful, to light an *actor* dark green, but a small amount of colour goes a long way in lighting a set effectively. Even if only a small area outside a window or low down behind a piece of scenery can be lit with colour the mood and atmosphere given to the whole scene is worth the effort. Using a cut-out filter or gobo to throw broken light on to a particular area of the scenery or floor is an effective way of creating mood and making a beautiful stage picture. Colour in lighting must, however, be used carefully, bearing in mind the colour of the scenery and costumes and even the actor's make-up, since certain colours change under coloured filters and certain chemicals in dyes and even washing powders, plus a variety of texture in the set, can alter the quality of refracted light.

Once the lighting is designed and the equipment hung, the operation of the LX cues during the show will depend on careful rehearsal. There will need to be technical rehearsals without actors, but with the SM and director, to set levels and timings, as well as further technical rehearsals with the SM and crew, and full technical run-throughs with the cast. Only then can there be anything like a dress rehearsal. Such occasions take time and tensions always run high. LX operators, even with computer boards to record cues, need to have patience and to train directors to allow time for everything to be set in the proper manner to avoid confusion. Nothing should ever be left to memory or inspiration and in the case of illness or emergency someone should be able to operate the lights from whatever system of cueing is in use.

Assignments

I Make notes concerning the following scenes about the actual cues, mood and setting of this piece. Imagine you are going to meet the director to talk over your ideas and also to discuss any questions you think need addressing.

Extracts from *Crucifer of Blood* by Paul Giovanni

SCENE ONE. PROLOGUE. (India. June 1857.) *The stage is black. A muezzin sings. Saffron coloured light from behind silhouettes the seventy-fifth gate of the Fort at Agra, India. The gate is an immense open arch with no doors . . . Through the arch of the gate, on the outside and only a few hundred feet away, the Taj Mahal glimmers in the half light. It is very hot. Two British officers,* CAPTAIN NEVILLE ST CLAIR *and* MAJOR ALASTAIR ROSS, *enter Stage Right . . . Both men are in their twenties.* ROSS *enters first, reading a large map by the light of a lantern.*

SCENE FOUR. *The Gate of a Hundred Sorrows – an opium den. The stage is dark. Music. A scream is heard. A match is struck illuminating the face of* ST CLAIR. *He sits on a pallet on the floor. The match is held by* FU TCHING, *a Chinaman, who steps upon a stool and lights an oriental lantern, which now reveals a large room.*
Across the back, cribs on which bodies are half visible, drugged and asleep in the shadows . . . On stage left a brazier burns.

SCENE FIVE. *On the River Thames. Inky blackness. A foghorn croaks. Fog hangs like a curtain over everything. A small police launch glides slowly out onto the stage. Only a lantern illuminates the faces of* WATSON, LESTRADE *and* HOLMES. *A* POLICEMAN *at the back steers the boat.*

From high up at the back of the stage two lanterns glow, one red, one green. They are fixed to the masthead of a large sailing ship which moves downstage; TONGA *a black pygmy scuttles back and forth, screaming and pointing to the men in the launch. He wears a frock coat and cape.* SMALL *comes out onto the prow of the sailing ship. He carries the chest. Putting it down, he leans over the rail of the ship.* TONGA *climbs up to the mast. The men in the launch rise and attempt to climb onto the schooner.* TONGA *takes out his blowpipe and puts it to his mouth. A dart hits the side of the ship.* LESTRADE *takes out his pistol and fires.* TONGA *falls, clinging to the mast over* SMALL'S *head. He groans in pain and then falls to* SMALL'S *feet.*

'An Opium Den' by Gustav Doré

2 Design and operate a pre-set sequence, that is to say a lighting sequence that sets the tone of the piece before the main action of the play begins. It should fulfil the following requirements:

A   Houselights down gradually.

B   Blackout.

C   The interior of a huge cathedral in South America. It is early morning.

D   A priest enters with a taper and lights candles on the altar. He blows out the taper and exits.

E   Other actors enter unseen by the audience and take up kneeling positions ready for the play to begin.

F   A procession of monks carrying banners, statues and sacred emblems enters, the cathedral becomes a blaze of light as the sun hits the stained glass windows and streams through the open door from the square outside.

Try this sequence in the round, as well as with a number of other arrangements of the space. Although sound would be an obvious adjunct to this play's opening moments, try to convey all the information and an effective stage picture with light alone.

SOUND

Sound is often under-used in the theatre. We are familiar with background music in film and television and there is a great deal of elaborate sound-mixing in stage musicals, but the theatre does not exploit the creative use of sound as much as it could. Most plays have some sound cues of a purely functional nature, but there are many opportunities for the addition of whole sequences of background or 'mood' sound which could add a whole new dimension to a play. This is especially important when limited scenery resources are available. Sound reproduction has reached great heights of sophistication while the equipment has become easier to use and less bulky. It is now possible, for example, to use long-running soundtracks for background effects and short cues for the timed effects.

As with stage lighting, the first requirement is to know one's equipment really well. It is very restricting to have to rely on commercially recorded sound effects, hired or bought for the occasion: good though these are, it is far better to mix them for oneself, and to use specially recorded sounds produced to order. Every good sound operator will want to be able to arrange a complete sound system to suit the particular production.

Many different systems of sound reproduction are available and methods are developing all the time. The safe use of all sound equipment depends on learning on the job. It may be necessary to go outside for tuition, since although the full range of equipment may not exist in other than a specialist centre (such as a recording studio), it could be essential to hire highly specialised equipment at some time and the sound operator will need to know how to use it. There is something to be said for using 'live' or hand-made sound in certain circumstances. (There is no recording of thunder to beat a well operated thunder sheet.)

Sound quality may vary from performance to performance, even in the same auditorium and with the same play. Changes in temperature, numbers in the audience and the energy levels of the players are all factors that can affect the sound quality, so that a pre-set level of amplification can become unpleasantly loud or almost inaudible. In such conditions it is very difficult to operate sound cues from anywhere but at the back of the auditorium, in the same acoustic as the audience, so that levels can be balanced as the performance proceeds.

Since sound equipment consists of microphones, amplifiers, speakers, cabling and control systems, the fitting out of a performance space can be a complex matter and may need not one, but several people, to form a department which is usually known as FX (for effects, whereas lighting is known as LX). Sound cue sheets are usually called FX sheets, even though they may cover much more than the normal range of 'noises off'.

Just like every other member of the production team, the sound operator will have to read the text, if there is one, prepare questions for the pre-production meeting, arrange the sound system to suit the space, and prepare material for a special meeting with the director for the exchange of ideas and the preparation of the exact number of cues.

Assignments

I There is to be a studio performance of *The Rose Tattoo* by Tennessee Williams with very little scenery other than a skeleton framework of a house. The director wants to use sound to convey atmosphere. Draw up a list of the exact cues mentioned in the extract from the script below and the sequence of sounds you might use in the background. Suggest the kind of atmosphere you are trying to create, and, if possible, collect some samples of the sounds you might mix to achieve the mood of the piece. You may even be able to make up complete soundtracks for both the background and the actual cues.

An extract from *The Rose Tattoo* by Tennessee Williams

The locale is a village populated mostly by Sicilians, somewhere along the Gulf Coast between New Orleans and Mobile. The time is the Present.

We see a frame cottage in a rather poor state of repair, with a palm tree leaning dreamily over one end of it . . . there are tall canes with feathery fronds and a fairly thick growth of pampas grass. These are growing on the slope of an embankment along which runs a highway which is not visible but the cars passing on it can occasionally be heard.

As the curtain rises we hear a Sicilian folk-singer with a guitar. He is singing.

It is the hour that the Italians call 'Prima Sera', the beginning of dusk

. . . The mothers of the neighbourhood are beginning to call their children home to supper in voices near and distant, urgent and tender, like the variable notes of wind and water.

GUISEPPINA.   Vivi! Vieni mangiare.

PEPPINA.   Salvatore! come home!

VIOLETTA.   Bruno! Come home to supper!

[*The calls are repeated tenderly, musically . . . A truck is heard on the highway.*]

ROSA.   Papa's truck!

2 Certain plays contain significant sound effects which may be quite unlike anything that has ever been heard before, or which have a certain significant meaning within the play. Create, record and play all the sound effects from the following extracts:

An extract from *The Cherry Orchard* by Anton Chekhov

[*They all sit deep in thought; the silence is only broken by the subdued muttering of* [the old manservant] FEERS. *Suddenly a distant sound is heard, coming as if out of the sky, like the sound of a string snapping, slowly and sadly dying away.*]

LIUBOV ANDRYEEVNA.   What was that?

LOPAKHIN.   I don't know. Somewhere a long way off a lift cable in one of the mines must have broken. But it must be somewhere very far away.

GAEV.   Or perhaps it was some bird . . . a heron, perhaps.

TROFIMOV.   Or an owl . . .

LIUBOV ANDRYEEVNA [*shudders*].   It sounded unpleasant, somehow . . .

[*a pause*]

FEERS.   It was the same before the misfortune: the owl hooted and the samovar kept singing.

An extract from *Brand* by Henrik Ibsen

GERD. Look. There he sits, the ugly brute. That's him.
Casting the shadow. Can't you hear him beating
The sides of the peak with his great wings?
Now is the moment, now! If only the silver will bite!

[*She throws the rifle to her cheek and fires. A hollow boom, like
thunder, sounds from high up on the mountain.*]

BRAND [*starts up*]. What are you doing?

GERD. I hit him. Look he's falling! Hear how he groans!
Look at his white feathers floating
Down the mountain side! Ah!
He's rolling down on top of us!

BRAND [*sinks exhausted*]. Must each man die to atone for human sin?

GERD. Look how he tumbles and rolls!
Oh, I shan't be afraid any more.
Why, he's as white as a dove! [*shrieks in fear*]
Oh the horrid, horrid roar!

[*throws herself down in the snow*]

BRAND [*shrinks before the onrushing avalanche*].
Answer me, God, in the moment of death!
If not by Will, how can Man be redeemed?

[*the avalanche buries him, filling the whole valley*]

A VOICE [*cries through the thunder*]. He is the God of Love!

An extract from a scenario for Jack and the Beanstalk

Jack returns to the giant's castle at the head of the beanstalk
and hides in the copper. He hears TWO sets of giant
footsteps, which shake the whole castle as they approach, then
the giant and his wife come in.
   'Fee-fi-fo-fum, I smell the blood of an Englishman!'
thunders the giant, his voice booming around the huge
kitchen. He sits at the table and eats and drinks a huge meal,
which he appreciates noisily. He then takes his magic harp.
'Sing, Harp!' orders the giant and the harp plays beautiful,

soothing music until the giant falls asleep, snoring giant snores.

Jack creeps, without more than a mouse's scratching footsteps, to the table and picks up the magic harp to make off with it, but the harp cries out in its harp's voice 'Master! Master!' The giant's snores turn to angry roars as he pursues Jack to the top of the beanstalk. Jack slides easily to earth but the giant falls straight down from the top with an agonising crash.

It would be interesting to try out various arrangements of audience, speakers and cross-fades, in order to 'move' the sound effectively about the space.

IV DESIGN

SETTING OR SCENE DESIGN

Like all other Theatre Arts, scene design is a close combination of technical skills and artistic ability. Stage sets have to be constructed very quickly, often to a limited budget and in a small space. They often have to be moved during a performance, they must be fireproof and safe, and capable of withstanding considerable activity. At the same time, the setting must convey the mood and living quality of the play as the director sees it and must be able to add not just a background but also artistry to a performance. Often when the curtain or the stage lights go up, there is a murmur or even applause for the set, before any actors have set foot in it. Some plays demand that the setting remains unremarkable, but for the most part theatre is not real life and an effective setting of something even as depressing as a derelict street can be both daunting and beautiful at the same time.

In the past, scene designers were often great landscape painters in their own right, but it is no longer absolutely essential to be able to paint pictures in order to paint scenery. The fashion of painting flat pieces of canvas to resemble a leafy glade or a palace interior is hardly ever seen in the theatre today, except in classical opera, ballet or pantomime. Even the job title has changed and scenic artists are now known as scene, or set designers.

There is a difference between setting and scenery in technical terms, however. 'Scenery' still means painted pieces, while the 'setting' for a play can mean levels and entrances or even a flat space with furniture. Setting a play also includes the work of the lighting, costume and sound departments and, above all, the director, so for the sake of clarity, the term 'scene design' will be used here. Scene designers are, however, part of a team. Because their work is part of the visual appearance of the production, they work closely with the lighting and costume departments, but because scenery takes a long time to build and is expensive, and because storage space is also too costly to allow a large stock of reusable items, the scene designer is usually the first of the visual artists to be asked to produce plans.

There are obvious difficulties in having to design the setting for a play before any work has been done with the actors, and, in the case of a devised piece, before any ideas are even forthcoming. The director may pass on very clear ideas about the setting, or alternatively may ask the designer to provide something more generalised or capable of being developed during rehearsals, but for the most part an early collaboration between the director and the design department is absolutely essential if any building is to be done.

As in all other Theatre Arts departments, there will be much work to do on the script or scenario beforehand. The scene designer will have some questions to ask the director about interpretation as well as about the technicalities of entrances, and levels, the actor/audience relationship in terms of space, and the style of performance. Questions of budget will also have to be settled at that meeting, so a careful reading of the play comes first, in order to establish the nature of the task. The designer can then make all the notes and any drawings that may be helpful at this stage.

In the professional theatre, models of the set are usually available at the first reading of a play. Rehearsals will take place on a marked out floor space and the actors may never set foot on the set until the technical rehearsal, so it is important that scene designers can not only visualise a set on paper, but are also able to make accurate scale models almost as soon as the play is chosen.

Some designers produce drawings, or a collection of magazine cuttings, photographs and sketches for the director at an early stage – this allows for a certain flexibility and changes in concept before any work goes into the final design, but other directors think better in three dimensions and it may be useful to play about with blocks and pieces of card made to scale, before assembling a detailed model. (A 'rough' model, made to no particular scale, is not helpful.)

Ground plans of the specific stage area may already exist, or may be available from the stage manager, and when making a finished, working model it is usually best to work to the same scale, unless it is impossibly small. Units of steps, flats or pieces of painted scenery, doors and even floors can then be set out on the plan and should be easily understood by everybody. The director and cast may be impressed by a model of the whole space, with an impression of the lighting coming from miniature spotlights, but in strict terms, all that is necessary is a well-constructed and accurately painted model of the setting which the designer can talk through at the first production meeting. There will also need to be working drawings for the workshop, carefully drawn to scale and an exact plan of the finished set with the measurements of every piece of scenery marked out on it. A model will not be enough, because the crew cannot stop to scale up something which, for example, may be shown on the model as a single unit but in reality is likely to be made from several flats.

Assignments

I Much of the time, a scene designer is asked to research and reproduce convincing architectural detail. One of the earliest scene designers in this country was Inigo Jones, the seventeenth century court architect. Look at the following drawings and make a model of the scene, showing how the pieces could have been arranged and moved. You may have to research into the methods used to stage court entertainments (masques) of the period.

Exterior view on p. 74 and interior on p. 75 of the Palace in the Rocks for Oberon *by Inigo Jones, 1611*

2 Your theatre space is going to be used for the performance of a festival of short plays. The organisers ask for a permanent set that can represent a medieval market place, a Hindu temple, a television studio and a dark forest. There will be only a few minutes between each playlet for changes of scenery or furniture. Make a model or sketches to talk through with the directors of each play.

COSTUME DESIGN

Sometimes setting and costumes are the work of the same designer, but this is rare in the theatre today. It is also possible for there to be two distinct areas of work; the wardrobe costumier who provides *clothes* to suit the actors and the roles they are to play, and the designer of *costumes* who is working out a complete visual image for the whole production, including a colour scheme and series of shapes. The best results are usually obtained when both functions are considered together. In other words, the director may specify that the actors' clothes should be as real as possible and should be bought ready-made, perhaps from jumble sales. Because the mood of the play is one of extreme bleakness and gloom, however, the designer may devise a colour scheme to unify the whole production and to fit in with the set design, and so will look for predominately purple and black garments.

Costume design, like scene design, combines both artistic and technical skills. Even if some well-known costume designers nowadays never cut a garment, in the early stages of a career in the theatre it will be essential to be able to make working drawings, to know a good deal about fabrics and to be at least conversant with the cut of period clothes. It will certainly be essential to be able to work to a budget, to have studied the history of costume and to be able to research and build up a portfolio of cuttings, drawings and photographs. Strangely, the ability to draw comes low on the list of priorities. Like the scene designer, there are many ways of conveying ideas to director, wardrobe and actors without being a first-rate painter, but most costume designers can at least draw a human outline and can think in terms of character, line and colour.

As with all other theatre departments, the costume designer needs to know the piece that is to be performed and to have questions for the director at a very early stage. It is also necessary to have a portfolio or collection of resource material which can be added to all the time.

Character

The eighteenth century actress, Sarah Siddons, once rejected a costume on the grounds that it was too original. She said, '. . . it is sufficient only that it be conventional'. What she meant was that the audience should be able to recognise a character immediately by the costume, and that there are certain conventions in dress by which we can tell a person's state of mind, such as black for mourning or pink for femininity. We may not like or agree with these conventions but they are the immediate handle by which a society unconsciously recognises types of character. Where stage costume is thought of in terms of *clothes*, then a study of character is the first priority. The designer and the actor must work together to help create the reality of a character. It is sometimes necessary for costume designs to be done so far ahead of rehearsals that the actors have to work on characterisation with a ready-made costume, and therefore with a predetermined image in mind, but, whatever the schedule, the best results are achieved by allowing time for consultation with the actors about characterisation as well as for costume fittings. It is never satisfactory for the actor not to know the costume before the dress rehearsal.

Line

The line of a costume is the way an audience immediately recognises period and style. The term means both the outline of the body as a whole as well as the lie of the material. The proportions of the human body often appeared completely different from one historical period to the next, so that the same person can be square in one costume and elongated in another. The designer should at least know how to recognise period line from documentary sources. Costume books with modern drawings are often excellent, but are always influenced by the artist's own style. It is better to research a number of original sources as well as finding out how to make the clothes from modern books. Patterns can then be taken with absolute assurance that you have the right period line.

Colour

A colour scheme for the whole costume design is most important. Nothing enhances the look of a play more immediately than a well thought out colour scheme, just as nothing is so confusing on the stage as a collection of clothes in random colours. Certain colours and fabrics were available and popular only in certain periods so that it immediately looks wrong to have 'chemical' colours in a period when natural dyes were the only ones available. It is worth repeating that the colour scheme for costumes and set design should be a matter of detailed consultation, just as it is important for the lighting designer to be included in discussions, so that an overall colour scheme for the production can be developed.

There are also practical considerations to be taken into account. Actors climbing steps, fighting, or even bleeding in a costume must have the ability to move easily and without damage to themselves or their expensive clothes. Set designers may have to take the width of a hoop or crinoline into account when designing doors or furniture, just as costume designers should take account of the set when designing the length of skirts or the height of shoes.

Assignments

I   The director of a promenade production of a devised piece, intends to base the characters on those shown in this print.

A Court for King Cholera

The casting will not be done for some time, but the director would like you to produce a colour scheme, fabric samples and some ideas for the range of garments that you suggest for this production, so that you can come to the first rehearsal and talk enthusiastically to the actors about the style of costume design you imagine being able to provide. (It might be possible to present your ideas verbally to others, and to answer questions if there are any. If it is a group project, you might each choose a different picture of a crowd scene on which to base your work.)

2 Design costumes for a schools tour of this show (see below). You have a minibus to carry the actors and costumes. There will be quite a lot of quick changes during the show. (NB: See also the mask design project on page 97.)

An extract from *The Blue Bird* by Maurice Maeterlinck

CAST LIST. MAIN CHARACTERS.

Mother Tyl.	Father Tyl.
Granny Tyl.	Gaffer Tyl.
Tyltyl.	Mytyl.

The Fairy Berelune./Neighbour Berlingot.

Neighbour Berlingot's little girl.

The Dog.	The Cat.
Bread.	Sugar.
Fire.	Water.
Time.	Night.
Sleep.	Light.
Death.	King of the Nine Planets.

LESSER CHARACTERS.

Hours. Ghosts. Wars. Stars. Nightmares.
Will o'the wisps. Fireflies. Perfumes of the Night.
Tall Blue Persons. Five Blue Children [and others].
Cow, Wolf, Rabbit, Horse, Bull, Sheep, Pig, Cock, Bear, Ass.
Pierrot, Pierette.

The Tyl family wear the dress of poor peasants in the fairy stories. Mytyl looks like Little Red Riding-hood; Tyltyl wears red knickerbockers and a blue jacket with white stockings. The Fairy also resembles a poor peasant although she may be transformed into a princess in the scene in Act One.

Dog resembles John Bull in Hunting dress. Cat wears black silk tights and spangles. Their heads are only discreetly animalised.

Bread wears a rich Pasha's dress with huge turban and scimitar, fat stomach and fat, red cheeks. Sugar is dressed in silk, as an Eunuch in a seraglio, half blue and half white with tall pointed headdress to resemble a sugarloaf.

The Dance of the Hours, Stars, and Elements [Fire, Night etc] in Grecian style.

STAGE PROPERTIES

The design and making of stage properties is a highly specialised job which is often undertaken by outside firms or by a separate department in the theatre workshops. There are also 'found props' which are all those objects on the set or handled by the actors which can be found or hired rather than made specially. Once a prop has been found or made, it becomes the responsibility of the stage management department, usually an assistant stage manager who is then 'ASM props'.

'Props' fall into three categories: personal props, which are those objects carried by the actors as part of their role or as costume accessories, hand props which are carried on to or handled on the stage and set dressings which are those that form part of the design of the scenery. There is sometimes a very fine dividing line between what is a prop and what is a piece of scenery, furniture or costume.

It would be a great pity if the work of the props department were ever thought to be unimportant. Because props are sometimes the last things to come on to the set, and sometimes added at a late stage of rehearsals, it might suggest that props are an afterthought. But it is because they are so significant that the decision about props is sometimes made as an integral part of characterisation, after costume and set have been designed. So the props designer must be an expert at making and finding props, and have the ability to work very fast.

Made props

Faking is essential, not just because the real thing may be too precious, but also because a fake often looks better or is easier to handle. Objects which would have been new and ordinary in the days when they were first made are now old and valuable. The props designer will have a great deal to learn about the tools of the trade and the methods of making and faking in glue and paint. Most of this can only be learned through practical experience, although there are now specialist books being written about what used to be a very traditional craft, and techniques in moulding synthetic materials or using newer kinds of glues are always being updated. Like the costume and set, props need both historical or geographical research and an eye for the potential in ordinary, even throw-away objects that could be remade into something of use for the stage.

Found props

Actors need to have props to rehearse with and therefore a supply of substitutes should be available in the rehearsal room. They will also need to know and be consulted about the end product. Consultation is essential, both with the director and the actors, about all the props in a show. Actors will sometimes say that they imagine a character having such-and-such, a pair of glasses or a walking stick or an old-fashioned handbag. It may be that they have the object themselves and will lend it, but, on the other hand, it may need an appeal among the cast or a search through junk shops and jumble sales to find the right thing.

All that has been said about reading the play and attending rehearsals, as well as consulting the other members of the design and production team applies as much to the props as to any other theatre designer.

For performances, a props table will need to be set up and maintained by the ASM in charge of props. The usual way of doing this is to cover a table with paper and draw round each of the objects in turn, writing in each space the name of the item. It is then very easy to see when any object is in place or has been carried on stage or mislaid. Two tables, one on each side of the stage, may be needed and actors will certainly need to be trained to replace props.

Assignments

1 Begin a portfolio of useful pictures by reproducing or collecting illustrations of the following:

(a) Jewellery to be worn at the coronation or wedding of the Emperor Napoleon.
(b) A set of utensils for a Tudor farmhouse kitchen.
(c) The contents of a secondary school stock-room in the 1950s.
(d) Personal props for the characters of Miss Marple and Hercule Poirot.

2 A children's theatre production requires the following things to be designed and made:

(a) A crown for King Throstlebeard (a rather sinister character).
(b) A superb banquet for one person.
(c) A grandfather clock with exploding works (to be reassembled on stage).

If possible, some or all of these should be made, or, if this is not possible, demonstrated in the form of working drawings or models.

V FACES

MAKE-UP

In the professional theatre, make-up is the responsibility of the individual actor. Only in film and television are there specialised make-up departments. The fact must be faced that there is less and less need for any make-up in the theatre. This is due to improvements in the level of lighting in most theatres and to the fact that most casting is done according to type. If a 60 year old actor is needed for a part then a 60 year old will be engaged.

In years gone by, actors might be engaged by a repertory company for a whole season and would have to play different roles every week or fortnight, but this system hardly exists any more so although young actors will have learned how to do a character make-up, they will very rarely have to do it.

The situation in schools and colleges, however, is very different. Here, young actors are often required to alter their appearance and there is a need for the skills to be learned and passed on; also, there is often less lighting on the stage area and so make-up may become more important. It is for these reasons that make-up and 'making faces' should be studied by everyone who is interested in Theatre Arts. It sometimes happens, however, that a student wishes to make a special study of make-up with a view to a future career in film or television make-up. It may also be necessary for a student to produce a design for the make-up of all the characters in a specific production, so the subject will be treated here as a design topic.

There are two distinct types of make-up material, one based on water and the other on oil. Sometimes, as in skin preparations generally, the two are combined as an emulsion, but, as may be seen in the following paragraphs, water-based or 'pancake' make-up usually produces a very different, and more unnatural effect from that of oil-based 'greasepaint'.

Naturalistic make-up

In order to achieve a realistic looking character, it is necessary to put something on your face that resembles the texture of normal skin. This is usually greasepaint which can be bought from a specialist firm. Make-up can be used to emphasise your own looks, to make your own face sadder, more sickly or more healthy according to the needs of the part; or it can be used to change character completely by blotting out a great deal of facial detail. Another face altogether is then imposed on top. By practising the technique of using greasepaint and by studying faces in paintings and from life, it is possible to achieve astonishing transformations. There is, however, nothing more absurd than a well-painted face that is not founded on a truthful performance. Actors should sit or stand in front of a mirror and look long and hard at themselves in character before beginning to put on any make-up. The thoughts and feelings that that character expresses will alter the carriage of the head and the way the eyes are shaped or the mouth is used, and any make-up must follow those natural lines or it will always look artificial.

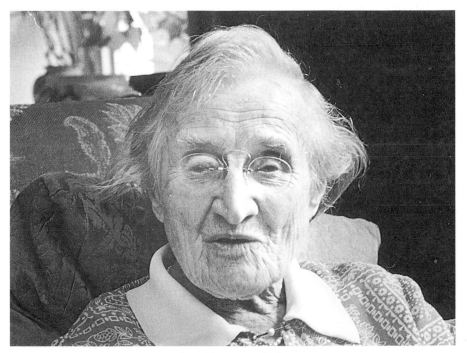

An old woman's face

Face painting

The whole purpose of face painting is to look as unreal as possible. Not that all characters are unreal, but people with painted faces, on stage or off, do look as though they are wearing make-up. A seventeenth century dandy, for example, would have painted his face white and used rouge and a beauty spot. Therefore the effect becomes somewhat stylised, just as a geisha girl wears a stylised face with a stylised costume.

Geisha girl in full make-up

There may also be a need to create an unearthly or mask-like look, and a water-based make-up, without any emulsified oils in it, produces an unnatural appearance that suits such 'beings' very well.

Water-based paint can also be used to good effect, in combination with greasepaint, on those parts of the body where grease would rub off, and as a base for other effects such as glitter or feathers which have to be glued to the face.

Preparation

On the basis that no make-up is better than overdone make-up, it is vital to think and plan carefully before designing a scheme for a whole production. In a naturalistic play, it will be very important to talk to the director and the actors about the way the characters are visualised, and to the costume and lighting designers about the way the play will appear to the audience. Coloured light can have a profound effect on make-up, and the whole appearance of a personality depends on the clothes and the face being part of the same visual image.

The make-up designer may have a sketch of a potential facial appearance that will help an actor towards projecting that character to an audience, so consultation late enough in rehearsals, when the character is beginning to emerge, is productive. A box file of mounted, near life-size, colour photographs or prints cut from magazines is a useful resource. Look at where changes in colour and skin texture are evident, at how the hair grows (moustache and beard if appropriate), where the natural lines occur, how the features of the face cast their own shadows and what colour those shadows are. Once the technique of using make-up has been mastered, a collection of faces is far more useful than a collection of make-up books, since your own files will contain material directly relevant to the range of skin colourings and features of your performance group and you will be able to help the actors towards a scheme that is based on their own needs. It is always useful to have a set of 'mugshots' of the cast, both in and out of make-up, for your own files and for future reference, and large reproductions of painted portraits show how some quite impressive variations of colour can exist side by side in one face.

Sketching may be a good way of fixing a make-up design in the mind, but it need not be more than a plan of the shapes and colours to be used. Pastel crayons on a rough paper are the best tools to use since the colours can be blended with the fingers, and it is possible to get hold of paper that is already the right base colour for black, brown, olive and pink faces. Drawings are essential for fantasy make-up.

Special effects, such as scars and blood can be bought from specialist firms and used with discretion, but all professional make-up, being specially manufactured to be safe as well as effective to use, is expensive and should not be wasted. It is always possible to add to the stock of professional stage make-up by collecting half-used eye-shadow and other make-up palettes, for the small amounts of blues and greys, etc. that may only be needed once.

Assignments

I Study this list of characters from the medieval play of *Everyman*. It is to be played in period costume in a church with some very effective white and pale-gold lighting. Design make-up for all the characters in the list.

An extract from *Everyman*

CHARACTERS

EVERYMAN	STRENGTH
GOD: ADONAI	DISCRETION
DEATH	FIVE-WITS
MESSENGER	BEAUTY
FELLOWSHIP	KNOWLEDGE
COUSIN	CONFESSION
KINDRED	ANGEL
GOODS	DOCTOR
GOOD-DEEDS	

HERE BEGINNETH A TREATISE HOW THE HIGH FATHER OF HEAVEN SENDETH
    DEATH TO SUMMON EVERY CREATURE TO COME AND GIVE ACCOUNT
    OF THEIR LIVES IN THIS WORLD AND IS IN MANNER OF A MORAL
    PLAY.

MESSENGER.   I pray you all give your audience,
            And hear this matter with reverence,
            By figure a moral play—
            The *Summoning of Everyman* called it is,

That of our lives and ending shows
How transitory we be all day.
This matter is wondrous precious,
But the intent of it is more gracious,
And sweet to bear away.
The story saith,—Man, in the beginning,
Look well, and take good heed to the ending,
Be you never so gay!
Ye think sin in the beginning full sweet,
Which in the end causeth thy soul to weep,
When the body lieth in clay.
Here shall you see how *Fellowship* and *Jollity*,
Both *Strength*, *Pleasure*, and *Beauty*,
Will fade from thee as flower in May.
For ye shall hear, how our heaven king
Calleth *Everyman* to a general reckoning:
Give audience, and hear what he doth say.

2 Make copies or tracings of these outline drawings and create a sad, happy and aged appearance on each one. You may be able to place colours under the outline on separate sheets of paper or you may have to make several copies and colour on top.

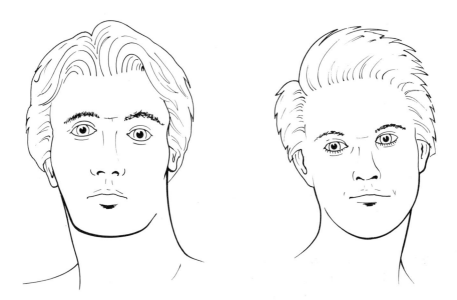

Outline drawings of faces

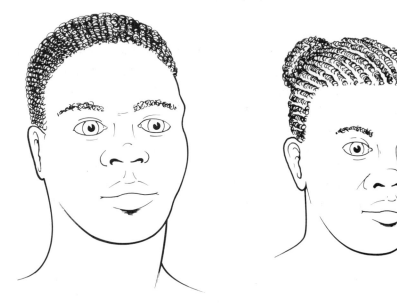

Outline drawings of faces

MASKS

Masks have acquired a symbolic and mystical importance over the ages because, unlike even the most stylised make-up, a mask is fixed, incapable of change and therefore gives the impression of a statue come to life. The use of masks changes not only actors' looks but also the way they move and speak. Wearing a mask often leads an actor to use ritualised movement and the physical quality of the voice is often changed by putting on a mask.

Just as the techniques of making masks are usually long and painstaking, mask-work in the theatre requires the actor to spend a good deal of time learning how to perform in a mask. It is therefore better to start with a very simple way of covering the head and face and to get used to a way of performing that suits the changed appearance of the actor than to concentrate on the many traditional ways of making masks. Very often a mask-maker can create a work of art which ends up as a beautiful wall decoration rather than as an adjunct to a theatre piece. In some cases it is possible for a set of masks to inspire the creation of a whole show, but in most cases it is the nature of the show that determines the kind of mask that is needed.

Simple first masks may be made by using metal foil purchased from craft shops, or even cooking foil doubled or quadrupled, or the type of fine mesh used in motor repair work. Any of these can be moulded straight on to the face and covered with layers of sticky paper or plaster bandage to produce quick effects. Whole heads can be built up on stapled card shapes or on wire frames that sit on the head or shoulders and can then be covered. Alternatively, a face mould can be taken by various means, from which all sorts of casts can be constructed, starting with the flexible and light latex mask to the PVA (polyvinyl adhesive) soaked felt, or even the traditional boiled leather mask of the Italian Commedia. There are so many different ways of making masks that the student has to find or invent the most appropriate for the time available and the style of the production.

Once the skill of making masks has been practised, then the pleasure of creating a set of disguises for the actors can begin. Masks can be utterly realistic (because they are based on the actor's face) and still look bizarre and unearthly, simply because they have fixed for ever one of the actor's normal expressions, or have created what seems a totally expressionless and therefore 'dead' version of the actor's face. A mask

Masked musician by Jacob Geyn

Bottom wearing a whole head mask – from A Midsummer Night's Dream, *Old Vic 1937*

can also, however, create the minimum disguise, perhaps by simply extending part of the face, like adding a pair of winged eye pieces or a hooked nose on a pair of glasses. Whatever the method, it is the exaggeration of the emotion or feature that gives the theatrical excitement. It is then up to the actor to give a convincing finish to the style and appearance of the image that has been created, by finding an appropriate scale of performance.

Masked dancers representing different aspects of the same character in
Anna Anna or The Seven Capital Sins

By far the most important factor in mask-work is the performer. The mask itself is merely an artifact until it is animated, yet many people misunderstand this and pay undue importance to the creation of the object without considering its part in ritualising emotion and the effect that it has on speech. In the huge arenas of Ancient Greece, where the characters in the drama were the legendary heroes of the remote past and therefore themselves outsize characters, the use of masks served both a practical and a symbolic purpose: practical because it enabled the audience to take in an outsize emotion over a large distance, and at the same time symbolic of the universal greatness of the characters involved.

A Greek tragedy mask from the 1st century BC

A great tragic performance where make-up reproduces the grandeur and horror of a classical mask: Laurence Olivier in Oedipus Rex

Assignments

Shut your Eyes or Turn Your Head

The cages have gone
Even the high mesh
Of the bird cage
Has disappeared.
Along with the penguins
And monkey and snakes
Went the jaguar, lion,
Leopard and elephant.
They all went together
At the same instant
That I shut my eyes.

If I shut my eyes
The words have gone
From the page,
So has the wall and door.
You too have gone.

Then I open my eyes
And in the zoo all round
I see folk in houses
In cars on television
On streets and in schools,
Everywhere I look
I can see people
Even in the cracks of the ceiling
Or outlined in clouds
Or beneath water,
In fire blaze.
And in this zoo
I see creatures caged.

Poor jaguar I would rather
Shut my eyes forever
Than see you forever caged.
But I must open them
Or I will bump into
What I cannot see.
Which proves perhaps
That I don't see everything
Even with eyes wide open.

I might bark my shins
On something obvious to you
Which I cannot see
Because I was looking
At something else.

There are many things
I'd rather not see I know
Some of them like the lion and jaguar
In the cage and people so jumbled
Together that they roll
Into a huge ball all arms and fingers
Clutching at something
That is never there.
I close my eyes to that.

John Fairfax

1 A dance drama is being rehearsed, based on the above poem. Design masks for some of the characters mentioned, particularly the lion and the jaguar. If possible, make and demonstrate the use of the masks.

2 Look up the costume design project on *The Blue Bird* (page 79). Either working with a costume designer or on your own, design, and if possible make a set of very simple masks for the play. Remember that the actors have to speak through the masks, that several touring performances will be given, and that quick changes will be necessary.

PUPPETS

Puppets can be used to create a miniature world, they can act as adjuncts to human actors or, like the outsize figures in a street carnival, they can make a gigantic impact.

An example of adult puppetry by the Bread and Puppet Theatre. Photograph © 1980 by Peter Moore.

The construction of puppets can be so elaborate that several people are required to operate one figure, or movements can be reduced to essential effects such as the sock placed over the hand to make an animal mouth. In all cases it is the skill of the operator that makes a puppet show successful. Throughout history, puppets have been used and have become an important artform because they have developed certain significant characteristics. For example, puppets can fly, go underwater and even disintegrate and come together again, thus undergoing legendary adventures of great fantasy and excitement. They can also multiply the skill of one or two operators, making it possible to travel with large cast plays where the 'actors' need neither to be fed or paid. This last consideration is no joke in places where villages are far apart and where the travelling puppet theatre is not just for children but an important social event in the life of any community that could never afford professional theatre.

Since, like other forms of theatre, performance and narrative skills are of great importance, a student should begin by using simple objects to tell a story and by communicating through the puppet in such a way that the audience forget that the operator is present and completely visible. To achieve such skill it is best to begin by attempting both silent scenarios and pieces of dialogue with such things as 'animated' dish or floor mops, coloured rope 'worms', or disjointed toys which have been restrung to make puppets. Some very successful scripts have been enacted using only several pairs of hands in white gloves appearing over the top of a screen.

After the fundamental operating/story-telling skills have been mastered, then the variety of historical puppets from shadow puppets to marionettes and carnival figures can be studied. Television has promoted another form of puppetry with the use of large figures superimposed on actors' bodies (as in *The Muppets* and *Spitting Image*). This technique has raised the artform from the traditional British view of puppets being only for children.

Following this research, it should be possible to start work on a story, which, in turn, will suggest an appropriate form of performance and the best method of construction. Like so many other Theatre Arts skills, the techniques of constructing puppets combine both science and art. The figures must have balance and flexibility; human and animal figures need to be anatomically sound; and the theatre in which they are to perform, even if it is a dark room in ultra-violet light, must be carefully thought out. A puppet show requires just as much attention to audience arrangement, focus, sightlines, sound, lighting and rehearsal as any other form of theatre. The only thing that may make the organisation simpler is that it is usually under the control of one or two people rather than a large team.

Artistically, puppet theatre relies heavily on visual appeal. Therefore, figures, their costume and scenery should be well finished and good to look at, besides being well designed.

Assignments

I Devise a script, or scenario, and use any form of puppet theatre you consider appropriate to tell your own version of this story to a group of fellow students. If possible, make and perform the show entirely by yourself or with one other assistant.

Fox and Stork by Aesop

Fox and Stork met one day beside the lake. Stork lifted his long beak out of the water and said, 'Good day'.

'Good day to you,' answered Fox with a low bow. 'And a very fine day it is. You're just the fellow I was looking for. Why not come along to my place this evening and have supper?'

'With pleasure,' answered Stork. 'I'll be with you at dusk.'

Now Reynard thought he would play a trick on Stork and make a fool of him. Then he could tell all the other animals about it, and show them what a clever fellow he was. He made some rich soup, and served it it in two shallow dishes. He took one himself, and set the other in front of Stork.

'I think you'll enjoy this,' said Reynard, as soon as Stork was ready for supper. 'Don't wait, my dear Stork, or the soup will be cold.'

He licked his own supper up with much enjoyment, and watched poor Stork trying to drink from the shallow dish with his long thin beak. Of course Stork had almost no supper.

'Aren't you enjoying it?' asked Fox.

Stork answered that he wasn't feeling specially hungry, and had really enjoyed his supper immensely. Before he went, he asked Reynard to come to supper with him the following day.

'With the greatest of pleasure!' answered Reynard.

Next evening, when Fox came to supper with Stork, he found that once more the meal was soup, and very good it smelt. But Stork had served it in two tall jars with narrow necks. Stork dipped his long beak into his jar, but Reynard got scarcely a drop and had to be content with licking the top. He was very angry indeed, and went home without saying good night.

But afterwards Reynard saw that he had been treated just as he deserved—and he did *not* boast to the other animals of how he had tricked Stork.

Those who play tricks on others must expect to be tricked themselves.

2 Choose a short passage of music and show how you could interpret it through various forms of puppetry. It should be possible to illustrate or describe the effectiveness of different techniques without making complete puppets, although it might be interesting to compile a video to demonstrate your ideas.

MULTI-MEDIA PERFORMANCES

Complete multi-media performances, or multi-media sequences as part of a show, have become quite commonplace. The term indicates the use of slides, projected images, film, shadow-play, lasers, holograms and other technical devices as part of a stage entertainment.

It is sometimes difficult to decide where to draw the line between the use of mechnical means of producing images and Theatre Arts, but it seems sensible to consider here only those visual images used as part of a theatrical representation, and not as a component in any other medium (such as video or film, for example), nor as a complete show without living performers. It is very possible to produce multi-media shows which, like firework displays, or 'son et lumiere', celebrate stories and events without any human intervention, but, for the sake of clarity, Theatre Arts is here defined as being 'any kind of performance rehearsed and prepared for presentation to an audience *and involving some form of human participation*'.

One of the chief reasons for using visual images, such as slides or film sequences in a play, is in order to give information. It is quite incorrect to believe that someone came on to the stage in Shakespeare's day with a placard saying 'In Another Part of the Forest'. Since many people in the audience could not read, it would certainly have been more effective to bring on a tree to show that the scene had changed. The truth is that such mechanical means are not needed on an open stage where the words alone serve to set the scene. A simple visual device, however, may serve to give information where words would be out of place. Lady Macbeth is sleep-walking and to let the audience know that she is dreaming rather than speaking aloud she enters carrying a candle. Such a visual shorthand can often be more effective than a long explanation, and in the theatre today there are many more sophisticated devices available to serve the same purpose.

In designing multi-media sequences for the theatre, it is important to think of the purpose first and the method only second. Information is not the only reason for using placards, banners or slides. A strong emotional effect may be achieved by presenting visual images in strong contrast to whatever else is happening on stage. Such an effect was achieved in Theatre Workshop's *Oh What a Lovely War* when picture and 'newspanel' slides were shown in conjunction with the offstage singing of soldiers and the mime of other soldiers digging graves. The irony of such a powerful combination is worth far more than any one image on its own.

Joan Littlewood's production of Oh What a Lovely War

Bertolt Brecht was one of the greatest exponents of the use of visual images as a contrast to the scene being played on stage (see the example below) and it is a field that is still open for experiment, especially in British theatre where, apart from musical theatre it is still an underdeveloped artform.

Bertolt Brecht production

Assignments

I This extract, translated into English from *Interior*, a short play by Maurice Maeterlinck, shows an unusual nineteenth century use of dumb-show or mime within a play. It might be possible to convey the effect of an audience watching another audience watching a silent play, by combining shadow-show, slides of paintings, still photographs or film, with actors. If it is not possible to stage the piece, make and show the 'interior' sequence and have someone read the actors' roles.

An extract from near the end of the one-act play *Interior* by Maurice Maeterlinck

One of the three daughters of the family has been found in the river, possibly having drowned herself, and the play is concerned with how to break the news to the family.

Scene, an old garden planted with willows. At the back, a house with windows lighted up. Through them a family is fairly distinctly visible, gathered for the evening around the lamp. The father is sitting by the fire. Mother, sitting in a large armchair, is resting one elbow on the table and gazing into vacancy. Two young girls sit at their embroidery, dreaming happily in the peaceful room. A child is asleep, his head resting on his mother's left arm. When one of them rises, walks or makes a gesture the movements appear grave, slow, apart, and almost spiritual because of the distance, the light, and the transparent film of the window-panes.

Murmured prayers are heard approaching the garden and a crowd files in, with deadened footfalls and whispering.

STRANGER [*to the crowd*]. Stop here. Do not go near the window. Where is she?

PEASANT. Who?

STRANGER. The others – the bearers.

PEASANT. They are coming by the avenue that leads up to the door.

The OLD GRANDFATHER *goes out.* MARTHA *and* MARY [*his granddaughters*] *have seated themselves on the bench, their backs to the windows in order not to see what is happening inside. Low murmurings from the crowd.*

STRANGER. Hush, do not speak.

In the room the taller of the two sisters rises, goes to the door and shoots the bolts.

MARTHA. Is she opening the door?

STRANGER. On the contrary, she is fastening it.

MARTHA. Grandfather has not come in?

STRANGER. No. She has returned to her mother's side. The others do not move and the child is still sleeping.

MARTHA. Give me your hand, Mary. [MARY *puts her arms round her. A pause.*]

STRANGER. He must have knocked . . . they have all raised their heads at the same time . . . they are looking at each other.

MARTHA. Oh! I cannot bear it.

STRANGER. He must have knocked again. The father is looking at the clock. He is getting up . . .

MARTHA. Mary, I must go in too . . . They can't be left all alone!

MARY. Martha, Martha! [*she holds her back*]

STRANGER. The father is at the door . . . he is drawing the bolts . . . he is opening it cautiously.

MARTHA. Oh! . . . You can't see the . . . ?

STRANGER. What?

MARTHA. The . . . the bearers . . .

STRANGER. He has only opened it a very little. I can only see a corner of the lawn and the fountain. He's kept his hand on the door . . . now he takes a step back and seems to be saying 'ah, it's you.' He closes the door again and your grandfather is in the room.

The crowd come up to the windows, followed by MARTHA *and* MARY. GRANDFATHER *comes in to the centre of the room. Everyone rises. The mother carefully settles the sleeping child in the chair and offers her hand to the old man, but withdraws it again. One of the girls offers to take his coat, the other pulls forward a chair for him, but he makes a little gesture of refusal and looks towards the window.*

STRANGER. He dare not tell them. He's looking towards us. [*murmurs in the crowd*] Hush!

The old man seeing faces at the windows quickly averts his eyes. He accepts the chair, sits and passes his hand over his forehead.

STRANGER.   He is sitting down.

The others also sit down while the father seems to be speaking volubly. At last the old man opens his mouth and seems to arouse their attention, but the father interrupts him. The old man begins to speak again and little by little the others grow tense. All of a sudden the mother rises.

MARTHA.   Oh! The mother begins to understand.

She buries her face in her hands. Renewed murmurings in the crowd. They elbow each other. Children cry to be lifted up. Most of the mothers do as they wish.

STRANGER.   Hush! he has not told them yet.

The mother is seen to be questioning the old man with anxiety. He says a few more words; then, suddenly, all the others rise and seem to question him. Then he slowly nods his head.

STRANGER.   He has told them! He has told them all at once!

CROWD.   He has told them! He has told them!

STRANGER.   I can hear nothing.

The old man also rises, and, without turning, indicates the door behind him. The family rush to the door which the father has difficulty opening. The old man tries to prevent the mother going out.

CROWD.   They are going out! They are going out!

Confusion among the crowd in the garden. All hurry to the other side of the house and disappear, except the stranger, who remains at the windows. In the room the folding door at the back is at last thrown open wide and everyone leaves at once. Beyond can be seen the starry sky, the lawn, and the fountain in the moonlight; while left alone in the middle of the room the child continues to sleep peacefully in the armchair. There is a long pause.

STRANGER.   The child has not wakened. [*He also goes out.*]

THE END

2 Make a stage documentary sequence using projected images taken from newspapers, with voices, music and, if possible, performers, based on some recent news events. The sequence need last only a few minutes, but consider how it might form part of a longer piece. (NB: If such a sequence were to be performed publicly there would be copyright considerations.)

BIBLIOGRAPHY

General Theatre Arts
Chris Hoggett (1975) *Stage Crafts*, A. & C. Black.
Francis Reid *The Staging Handbook*, Pitman.
Trevor R. Griffiths (1982) *Stagecraft*, Phaidon.
Thompson and Salgado (1985) *Everyman Companion to the Theatre*, J. M. Dent.

Acting
Litz Pisk (1975) *The Actor and His Body*, Harrap.
Cecily Berry (1973) *Voice and the Actor*, Harrap.

Directing
Peter Brook (1972) *The Empty Space*, Penguin.
Clive Barker (1977) *Theatre Games*, Methuen.

Lighting
Francis Reid (1976) *The Stage Lighting Handbook*, Pitman.
Frederick Bentham (1976) *The Art of Stage Lighting*, Pitman.
Richard Pilbrow *Stage Lighting*, Studio Vista.

Sound
Graham Walne (1990) *Sound for the Theatre*, A. & C. Black.
David Collison (1976) *Stage Sound*, Pitman.

Design
Lucy Barton (1961) *Historic Costume for the Stage*, A. & C. Black.
Motley (1964) *Designing and Making Stage Costumes*, Studio Vista.
Michael Warre (1966) *Designing and Making Stage Scenery*, Studio Vista.

Make-up
Bert Broe (1984) *Theatrical Make-up*, Pelham Books.
Phillippe Perrottet (1967) *Practical Stage Make-up*, Studio Vista.

Masks
Chester J. Alkema (1981) *Mask Making*, Ward Lock.

Properties
Jaquie Govier (1984) *Create Your Own Stage Props*, A. & C. Black.
Warren Kenton (1974) *Stage Properties and how to make them*, A. & C. Black.

Experimental Theatre
James Roose-Evans (1970) *Experimental Theatre*, Discus Avon.
John Willet (1978) *The Theatre of Bertolt Brecht*, Methuen.
Ann Jellicoe (1987) *Community Plays: How to put them on*, Methuen.

Theatre History
Diana Devlin (1989) *Mask and Scene*, Macmillan.
Bamber Gascoigne (1968) *World Theatre*, Ebury Press.

ACKNOWLEDGMENTS

The author wishes to acknowledge the help given to her over many years by Stephen Webber, Donald Walker and the staff of the Curtain Theatre.

The Publishers would like to thank the following for permission to reproduce material in this volume:

Abner Stein and Samuel French Inc for the extract from *The Rose Tattoo* by Tennesee Williams (1950); The Bodley Head for the extract from *The Love Girl and the Innocent* by Alexander Solzhenitsyn, translated by Nicholas Bethell and David Burg; Faber and Faber Ltd for the extract from *Waiting for Godot* by Samuel Beckett; Grafton Books for the extract from *Brand* by Henrik Ibsen, translated by Michael Meyer; John Fairfax for his poem 'Shut Your Eyes or Turn Your Head' from *Poetry 4* edited by Moira Andrew (1987); Penguin Books Ltd for the extract from *The Cherry Orchard* by Anton Chekhov, translated by Elisaveta Fen (Penguin Classics, 1951), © Elisaveta Fen, 1957; Samuel French Inc for the extract from *Crucifer of Blood* by Paul Giovanni (1979).

The Publishers would also like to thank the following for their permission to reproduce copyright photographs in this book:

Agence de Presse, p.17; The Ancient Art and Architecture Collection, p.94b; Artia, p.92; La Bibliotheque Nationale, p.20 t. & b.; Devonshire Collection / Chatsworth, reproduced by permission of the Chatsworth Settlement Trustees, pp.74, 75; Gordon Fraser Gallery, p.12; Bamber Gascoigne, p.28 t. & b.; Sally and Richard Greenhill, p.85; Robert Harding, p.86; Herzog Anton Ulrich-Museum, p.26; The Hulton Picture Company, p.35; Mander and Mitchenson, p.93; The Mansell Collection, pp.14, 65; Roger Mayne, p.21; Peter Moore, p.98; The National Szechenyi Library, p.15t.; Inter Nationes, p.105; Popperfoto, p.18; Punch Publications, p.78; Theatre Notebook / Society of Theatre Research, p.8; Theatre Royal, Stratford East, pp.103, 104; The John Vickers Theatre Collection, pp.57, 95.

Every effort has been made to trace and acknowledge ownership of copyright. The Publishers will be glad to make suitable arrangements with any copyright holders whom it has not been possible to contact.

Unless otherwise acknowledged, play extracts have been devised or translated by the author.